Gypsy Boy

Gypsy Boy

Mikey Walsh

HODDER &
STOUGHTON

Publisher's Note
Mikey Walsh is a pseudonym. All names and other identifying
details have been changed to protect the privacy of Mikey's family.
Some characters are not based on any one person but are composite characters.

First published in Great Britain in 2009 by Hodder & Stoughton
An Hachette UK company

I

A CIP catalogue record for this title is available from the British Library

Hardback ISBN 978 0 340 97796 5
Trade Paperback ISBN 978 0 340 97797 2

Typeset in Sabon MT by Palimpsest Book Production Limited,
Grangemouth, Stirlingshire

Printed and bound in the UK by CPI Mackays, Chatham ME5 8TD

Hodder & Stoughton policy is to use papers that are natural, renewable
and recyclable products and made from wood grown in sustainable forests.
The logging and manufacturing processes are expected to conform to the
environmental regulations of the country of origin.

Hodder & Stoughton Ltd
338 Euston Road
London NW1 3BH

www.hodder.co.uk

To Leigh

Acknowledgements

I would like to thank the following people for making this book possible:

To Caro Handley, for being so patient and always on my side. To Stephanie Thwaites, for your guidance and support. And Fenella Bates . . . I often wonder how things would have gone if you had never opened my submission. Without your belief in my writing this piece would never have become possible. A mere thank you seems so little a compensation for the magnificence of who you are and what you have done for me. There are no words I can find that express what all this means. I wish you everything.

And then there are those that have been listening to my story for years:

To Mr C and your wonderful Green. To Mr Robert Caton . . . 10 years. Will we still be quoting lines from He-Man cartoons when we are seventy? To my sister, for teaching me how to pull off a floral nightie and red stilettos. To My Little "Big" brother. You're a hero in every sense of the word. May you never tell of this book. To my brilliant mother. May you never hear of this book. To my wonderful friends who put up with me so well – you know who you are. To my new Aussie family. Thank you for being so marvellous. And thank you Nan, for the Legs of lamb and trivia.

To my ball and chain. I love you Always.

To all those other Kids of the 80's . . . Never Say Die.

And last of all, to you who read this book. I wrote this just for you.

Mikey

Contents

I

The Birth of a Pig Boy

They were travelling through Berkshire with the rest of their convoy when my granny Ivy's water broke in the back of a van. Most Gypsy women in those post-war days would give birth at home with the help of other women but, being less than four feet tall and easily mistaken for a pygmy in a cardigan, Ivy, despite having the temperament of an ogre, was in no condition to have a home birth without the aid of a real nurse and a couple of doctors.

The nearest hospital was the Royal Berkshire, and Ivy had no choice but to go there for the birth of her child. She successfully popped out a strapping boy, Tory, and within a couple of years she was back there, this time producing twins: my father Frank and his sister Prissy. Ivy's youngest and most precious, Joseph, arrived another two years after that.

Ivy and my grandfather, Old Noah, were Gypsy royalty and the dedication that the Royal Berks bestowed on one of the Gypsies' best-known elders was not forgotten. By the time Joseph arrived, just about every new baby in the Gypsy community was being born there.

Reading is a sprawling town just outside London with no major landmarks or attractions, but its status as home to the Royal Berks made it the most popular Gypsy destination in the country. Wherever they were, when the time to give birth drew near, travelling families would flock to one of the many campsites surrounding the town.

When my own turn came, the moment was witnessed by my father, Granddad Noah, Granny Ivy, my other granny, Bettie, my mum's sister, Aunt Minnie and her husband Uncle Jaybus. Births, like weddings and funerals, were a shared event in the Gypsy world, and this one all the more so, not only because my mother had a heart murmur and there were fears for her health, but because the family were fiercely determined that she would deliver them a boy.

My parents already had a daughter, my sister Frankie, so this baby simply had to be my father's longed-for first son.

As I was laid in my mother's arms, Granny Ivy, with her dyed black bouffant hair, mouthful of gold teeth and the physique of that of a child said 'That is the fattest child I have ever seen in my life, Bettie! A little pig boy.'

The heads around the bed cackled, nodding and stroking their chins in unanimous agreement.

I have no idea what I weighed – or what I looked like – but the night Bettie Walsh gave birth to a pig has gone down in family folklore.

For years my mother would brag that I near killed her. I spent my childhood listening to Gypsy women cluck and howl about the day Bettie brought her oversized piglet home. If there had been a prize for the biggest, ugliest, fattest baby, I would have been awarded the biggest, ugliest, fattest trophy. And, after the number of times I had to sit and politely listen to the story of how horrified they were at the sight of me, I felt I deserved one.

The first thing my father did, in the minutes after I arrived, was to place around my neck a gold chain with a tiny pair of gold boxing gloves on it. It had been made before they even knew what sex I would be; a symbol of my future glory, and my father's highest hopes.

In each country, there is one man that wears the crown in the sport most favoured by Gypsy culture: bare-knuckle fighting. This crown is the Holy Grail amongst Gypsy men, but whether they go for the crown or not, all Gypsy men will have to fight as part of their day-to-day life. It would be impossible for any Gypsy man, no matter how much he might wish for a quiet life, to be in the company of other Gypsy men without being asked to put his hands up. And when he is asked, that is what he must do. No matter how little chance he has of winning, he must defend his honour, even if he will simply end up a bloody and battered notch on the belt of an aspiring fighting man or, more often, a two-bob bully.

Any man who aims for the crown has to fight – and beat – a host of others to get there. And the life of a true Gypsy champion is a tough one. The price that comes with the title is that he must spend his whole life fighting to retain it, for there is always a new, eager and younger contender waiting to take his place.

That's why our family was considered special. The bare-knuckle crown had been in our family since my great-grandfather, Mikey, first won it.

He had moved to Britain from Eastern Europe during the Blitz, poverty stricken and homeless, with his wife and their children: three sons and two daughters. The war had almost finished off the Gypsies, who were loathed and persecuted by the Nazis. Many in Europe were convinced that we had been wiped out, and would survive only as a mere footnote among the other cultures that had fallen prey to the Holocaust. But some defied the odds, and in the years after the war, they regrouped and built up their communities once again.

When my great-grandparents moved to Britain, Mikey and his wife Ada did whatever they could to make a living. She hawked good-luck charms and told fortunes, while he fought for money, putting up his fists for anyone who would throw in a few pounds. The two of them prospered, and Mikey's reputation as a champion fighter grew.

They earned enough to buy a piece of land. And they turned that land into a home; a camp for Gypsies, to take them off of the roadsides, farmers' fields and lay-bys. They offered affordable rents, good company, a place to keep animals and shelter from the prejudices of the outside world. Gypsies flocked to live on their site.

The need to fight for money had gone, but the lust for blood and the thrill of victory had not. And so, it became Mikey's fate to fight on. Every bold young Gypsy man in the country, thirsty for glory, came to try his luck against the champion. And he beat them all until, after years of undefeated bliss, he finally became too old to compete with younger, stronger men and was beaten. His son Noah, still only a boy and too young to fight, swore to earn his birthright back. And at the age of sixteen, he did just that, grinding the man who had defeated his father into the ground.

Determined to keep the crown in his family, Noah brought his sons up to be gladiators amongst Gypsies.

From the earliest age he forced his boys to fight grown men and even each other, until they learned to be fearless and ferocious.

'Hit 'em so they'll never get back up. One. Good. Hit. Put out your man like a candle,' he would repeat. It became his sons' mantra.

By the time my father had reached his teenage years he had beaten just about every man worthy of fighting in the whole country. He longed for the title and the respect and praise from his father that would come with it. But the crown my father was desperate for had already been won by Tory, his older brother; not only the best fighting man amongst Gypsies, but also richer and more handsome than my father and the unshakeable favourite of their father. So successful was he that he went on to become a boxing champion in the non-Gypsy world too.

My father stood no chance against his brother and, with his own hopes frustrated, he pinned them on his son, determined that I would be the fighting man to beat all others, including Tory's two strapping boys, young Tory and young Noah, who, though little more than toddlers themselves, were already shaping up to be prize specimens.

My impressive size and ugliness at birth only served to fire my father's enthusiasm. And once the chain, with its golden gloves was around my neck, he wanted a fitting name for me.

My mother didn't fancy the popular Gypsy names like Levoy, John, Jimmy, or Tyrone. Hooked on the eighties glamour of her favourite TV show, *Dynasty*, she was stuck on naming me Blake. My father and his family were not, especially Old Noah.

'That's a fucking ugly bastard of a boy that is,' he told my parents. 'You can't call him Blake.'

My mother was quite accustomed to the harsh bluntness of her father-in-law, but that was a step too far. She remained adamant that my name should be Blake – until my father stepped in and insisted I be named after his grandfather, the grand old prizefighter, Mikey.

So Mikey became my official name. But to my mother, I was always, and always will be, Blake.

With the name sorted, or at least compromised on, they took me home. My mother had brought a wicker basket, in which she placed me, but it wasn't up to the job of holding such a bruiser of a baby. As she carried me out of the hospital, I ripped through the bottom of the thing and bounced down the front steps to the pavement below.

'You didn't make a sound,' my mother said, as she recounted the incident to me some years later. 'I ran down the steps, screaming after you and you had your face flat into the ground, totally silent. I thought you were dead. But when I turned you around, you looked as if I'd just woken you from a deep sleep.'

I was rushed back in, and checked over, but found to have only a few grazes. I was considered very lucky. But by the time my mother and father had got into the car to take me home, they had begun to get concerned.

'He's not made a sound, Frank.'

'He's a mute. I bet on my mother's life, I've got myself a mute child,' my father said.

Home was a caravan park just a few miles outside Reading. Ours was one of a circle of trailers, all with small gardens and a shed behind. The central area, where the trailers faced one another, had been intended as a play area for children, but over the years had become a dumping ground for old cars with most of their engines and insides ripped out. The little garden areas behind the trailers were the same – heaped with car parts, old cars, rubbish and scrap. Most of the men made their money from putting cars together from the assorted bits scattered about or selling the spare parts. By the time I arrived the place was so heaped with scrap that there was barely enough room for us to drive through the gate, negotiate the car through the mountains of rubble, and park behind our trailer.

This was not the land my great-grandparents had bought. That had been sold to buy Tory a grand house, a second-hand car dealership and a scrapyard, which he ran with his youngest brother Joseph.

The inside of our trailer was typical of an early eighties caravan – chocolate brown mixed with a slap of bright, Halloween orange. The couch was embroidered with different shades of autumnal flowers, the walls, although they looked wooden, were actually cheap fibreglass panels that were easily broken and bore testament to my father's temper. There were several jagged portholes the size of his fist, and one huge head-sized one in the wall between the kitchen and the lounge, which looked like a jagged diner window. Around the walls there were family pictures and plenty of the gilt-edged mirrors so beloved of Gypsy women. My mother was never a sovereign-earrings kind of Gypsy and she wasn't keen on the gilt, but she did find that the mirrors were useful for disguising the 'architectural flaws'.

My sister Frankie, then almost two years old, was delighted to find she had been brought a new toy. But as my silence continued over the following weeks my parents became increasingly concerned. I didn't cry, gurgle or make any baby noises at all; I just lay there wide-eyed, looking up at the ceiling. They began to wonder what on earth could be wrong. Unable to tell when I was tired, hungry, or just plain agitated, Mum and Dad took turns watching my cot.

By the time I had learned to sit up on my own, at six months, apparently I still hadn't made a sound. But everything changed the day my mother brought home a colossal crab. They were her favourite snack, and once a week she would bring home a good, brick-sized one, complete with face, from her regular Friday shopping trip. One day she propped me up on some pillows and placed one of the – thankfully dead – beasts in front of me while she finished her cleaning. At first, I just stared, mystified. But eventually I became a little braver, I reached out and poked it; then rolled it over, and finally picked it up. After that the little sea monsters fascinated me so much that, to my mother's joy and relief, they caused me to grunt and squeal with excitement every time she placed one on my lap. I never lost my fascination for them, and by the time I was two I had learned to dissect the body and even to work the mechanism for its pincers.

By the time I was two or three and old enough to play, Frankie had become my best friend and heroine. We looked like twins. The only real difference was in the colour of our eyes; Frankie's were near black in colour, just like our mother's, while mine were bright green, like Grandfather

Noah's. Both of us had olive skin – though hers was a little darker – and thick dark hair. Mine, was styled into the typical helmet look of an eighties street kid, while Frankie's bounced in thick black curls like a Latino Shirley Temple.

Granny Bettie hated Frankie's hair. She thought a proper Gypsy girl's hair should be straight as a poker and long enough to sit on.

One day, when she was looking after us, after telling her that her hair made her look ugly, she handed Frankie a pair of scissors and left her alone in her bedroom. She knew full well what would happen, and by the time our mother came home, Frankie had lopped off every curly ringlet.

After that she had to wear a hat for a while, which suited her tomboyish nature, and meant that the adults in our camp would often mistake her for me.

There were a few other children on the campsite that we played with, but mostly it was just Frankie and me, and we liked it that way.

We did hang out on occasion with a pair of real twins, Wisdom and Mikey. They were cousins of ours. Although they were twins, Wisdom and Mikey looked absolutely nothing like one another. Mikey, who was also named after our great-grandfather in the hope that he would inherit some of the legendary fighting spirit, had a permanent squint and the grimace of an old lady with a smoker's mouth, while Wisdom had an extremely narrow head and was constantly picking off the slab of snot that crusted around his upper lip.

We played He-Man together, using sticks and dustbin lids, but the twins were eventually banned from playing with us because Frankie would always get too rough. She even killed their pet rabbit by beating it to death with a broom handle. She didn't mean to – like me, she loved animals – but unfortunately she got overexcited and was never able to comprehend how much pain she was causing.

When Frankie and I played together she was always in charge. Her favourite pastime was dressing me up as her Aunt 'Sadly'. We were both fans of *Worzel Gummidge*, but neither one of us could pronounce Sally properly. Aunt Sadly ran a shop that sold lovely clothes, make-up and babies. I would dress up in Frankie's night gowns and set up shop in our room, with Frankie's army of Cabbage Patch dolls – all provided by Old Noah, who bought her a new one every week – as the babies.

Frankie would get dressed up, plaster herself with the various shades of brown and orange make-up that she would steal from Granny Bettie, pop into Aunt Sadly's shop to hang around for a gossip before choosing a child to take home.

Frankie liked to make meals for her Aunt Sadly too, and invite her over to eat. Her specialty was a raw egg, mud and Play-Doh pie, which I dutifully did my best to eat without vomiting over the front of my dress.

We loved these games and played happily for hours, though never when my father was around. He was not keen on Aunt Sadly at all. And he wasn't alone in disapproving. In Gypsy culture boys and girls are kept apart. Frankie was always dressed like a china doll: little dresses, ringlets and diamond earrings, which she hated, while I was in a miniature version of an old man's togs; a flat cap, dungarees and, of course, the chain with the gold boxing gloves that

I could never take off, not even in the bath. Right from the start, boys and girls are expected to inhabit different worlds, and I soon learned that, even by the age of two or three, already my path had been chosen for me.

2

Wonder Years

My parents were, in many ways, typical Gypsies. My mother, like all Romany Gypsy women, kept a proud, clean home and looked after the children. Gypsy women were not allowed to work outside the home, the only exceptions being the handful that occasionally sold trinkets and told fortunes.

Gypsies are very superstitious people; black cats are seen as a good sign, as are horseshoes, and even Dalmatian dogs, as long as you can spit on both hands and rub them together before you lose sight of one. They are also certain that if a bird flies into your home, someone is about to die. But contrary to popular belief, they don't believe in magic, and the Gypsy 'curse' is no more than an age-old way of scaring non-Gypsies into buying something.

I have run into many people who have asked me to remove a curse placed on them by a Gypsy, because tradition says that it can only be removed by another Gypsy. Of course I oblige. I may not believe in curses, but the poor people who have suffered at the hands of some old Gypsy woman often do.

My father did a bit of this and a bit of that. Sometimes it was scrap metal – collecting it, weighing it, then selling it on. At other times he'd do casual work, such as laying tarmac. Then there were the 'grunters': old people whom my father would visit, offering to do 'essential' jobs, like cleaning their gutters, fixing their roofs or resurfacing their drives. He would charge ridiculously large sums of money for small and often unnecessary jobs. Grunters were considered fair game, because they were Gorgias: non-Gypsies.

Most Gypsies despise all Gorgias. They believe they are only good for making money from. The old people were the best targets because they were easy to find, and to con. Some of the Gypsy men would go back time after time to the same old person until they'd stripped them of their last penny.

As a small boy I remember seeing old men and women crying to my father as they stood on their 'new' driveways, telling him that they just couldn't afford to pay the amount he had asked. But my father showed no remorse, demanding his money and sometimes even driving them to the bank and waiting while they took out what little money they had left.

'I have a family to support,' was his line. 'They're on the way out, they don't need their money.'

My father's reputation as a great con man almost surpassed his family's infamy as fighting men. His family, once well respected, had come to be feared. Wherever they went the Walsh men were always bristling for a fight, prowling the campsites and Gypsy nightspots, scouting for easy victims, and demanding that any man who looked at them the wrong way put up his fists. They had no real friends, just a handful of fans and endless amounts of troublemakers and fiends who trailed after them, fuelling their already over-bloated egos.

My mother, Bettie, was a friend of my father's twin sister Prissy – the two of them had been friends and smoking buddies since they were ten years old. Prissy was born with illness in her bones, and in her later life she would need to use a wheelchair. But even with crippling arthritis, she was as fiery as the rest of the Walsh clan; a typical, dark-skinned Gypsy girl, with tar-black hair that fell about her hips, eyes as green as a ripe amphibian, and a cigarette permanently dangling from her lip.

The cigarette was the only thing the two girls had in common, because my mother couldn't have looked more different. She somehow emerged from her dark-skinned mother with milk-white skin and flaming red hair. She was a curiosity and an embarrassment to her family who couldn't understand where this unusual creature came from. Some people even muttered about a curse – Gypsies don't believe they can curse others but a few believe they can be on the receiving end of one. In truth, though, she was just different, both in her looks and in her temperament. Unlike most Gypsy women she hated gossip, and was happy spending time alone.

She was the second oldest of six children, her older brother taking her father's name, Alfie, and she her mother's. Her mother, Bettie, was an old battleaxe with legs that were the same width all the way down. She was a chronic hypochondriac and had a permanently constipated look on her face. Mum's father was a handsome old devil with a dark sense of humour. He had multiple sclerosis and a reputation for being an old loon that he played up to, just for laughs. He couldn't stand fighting and he didn't like horses either – another Gypsy passion – and he only cared for a dog if it was under the wheel of his lorry. He was very keen, though, on inventing various stews; his favourite was a whole pig's head, dropped in a barrel of gravy and potatoes.

Alfie and Bettie and their brood lived on their own plot of land: an over-grown field with two trailers and a huge double-decker bus, splashed with a rainbow of colours. The bus had been a Christmas present one year to the kids, who had woken to find one clapped-out bus and eight cans of paint.

Behind the field were the woods, and hidden in them, what Alfie described as his 'plantation'. He grew drugs – strictly medicinal, he insisted – which after several 'tests' would be sold on to local hippies . . . and even local police officers.

The whole clan, apart from my mother, were dark-skinned, dark-haired and of Granny Bettie's hefty build.

My mother always told us that she fell in love with our father when she first laid eyes on him at the age of ten. And he fell in love with her too despite, or perhaps because of, her unusual looks; he knew she was the woman he wanted. Unfortunately for her, the only way he knew how to talk was by punching someone in the teeth. When he wasn't fighting he was tongue-tied with shyness. So much so that he was too frightened to come near her for three years. Instead, he would beat up every travelling man who so much as stood close to her. He punched a male cousin of hers in the mouth, smashing the poor man's teeth out, just because he'd escorted her into a bar.

My father's refusal to let another man come near her, while not actually speaking to her himself, left my mother high and dry. Eventually she did the unthinkable, in Gypsy society, and approached him.

Her opening line left a lot to be desired, but it did the trick.

'Are you going to ask me out or what? If not, will you just fuck off!'

My father, thus confronted, found his tongue and asked her out. And that was it. As the stories have it, he only cheated on her once, which led to my mother, her sister Minnie and his own sister Prissy, writing several unsavoury swear words all over his new car in lipstick: a nightmare to clean off, apparently.

After a year of courting, my mother accepted my father's bumbling proposal and, at eighteen, they got married. She wore a white wedding dress that was, typically, non-traditional. We would always refer to it as her 'Mary Poppins at the fair' outfit. And it was – complete with a hat with a candy-coloured ribbon and parasol. My father, on the other hand, showed up in the same clothes he had worn the night before: beige corduroys, an ill-fitting grey checked cardigan, the usual clump of garish gold on each finger, and a rose shoved in his breast pocket. There isn't a photo of the wedding in which my mother doesn't look furious.

Despite that the two of them loved one another very much. He loved her for being so different: her small, svelte frame and calm voice. She saw his sensitive side and understood the troubled boy within him and his need to prove himself to his family.

Within months she was pregnant. Both families were convinced that an heir was on the way, but my mother gave birth to a girl, and shortly after was told she had a heart murmur and that it could be fatal if she were to attempt to have another child.

Crushed, my father tried to accept his ill-fate, relishing the birth of his baby girl, and even giving her his own name, Frank, which he had been saving for his first boy. But a longing for a boy festered within him and he began to beg my mother to try again. Less than a year later she consented, favouring my father's happiness over the risk to her own life.

She fell pregnant once again and I arrived with, thankfully, no sign of trouble from her heart. We spent a lot of time with our mother because our father was often away for days at a time, up to goodness knows what 'business' with the other men. Most of it was dodgy, but he made good money – we certainly weren't poor. Contrary to popular belief, not many Gypsies are. Our clothes were clean and well made and we had all that we needed and plenty to eat. We lived mostly on take-out food and we all preferred it. Mostly because our mother's cooking was never her strong point. She did her best though; beans on toast, just toast, or a bowl of canned soup. Apart from the occasional attempt at a Sunday roast, the only time she cooked a big meal was when she made the pig's head stew she had learned from her father, which she always followed with jam roly-poly and custard to take away the bad taste in our mouths.

She filled the kitchen cupboards with easy-to-prepare food: Rice Krispies and Frosties, pot noodles, crisps and the thick slabs of bread and butter we ate with every meal. We also had copious amounts of salt; whatever was served up, our father would usually have more salt than food on his plate, often using several spoons of it on a single meal.

Both our parents had an incredibly sweet tooth and our mother would often live on a Mars Bar a day and nothing else. She always had a tin of sweets around the trailer and she would help Frankie and me make Angel Delight, a 'just add water' dessert we all had a big thing for.

Although we had a table in the kitchen, most of the time we only used it to mix up our sticky concoctions. We ate our meals off our laps in front of the TV, unless it was a takeaway, in which case Frankie and I ate in the back of the cab of our father's lorry, while listening to our parents bantering in the front.

My father was very dark, with a stout, barrel-shaped body and short, stubby legs. Our mother always had to take his jeans and trousers up; he liked them taken up too much so that you could see his socks. In his eyes, it made him look taller. He was solid, with hands as huge as spades, dried out and rough as sandpaper. His palms were full of open cracks, like severely parched land. He had dark brown eyes, with yellow whites and they had dark rings sunk deep around them, making them protrude and giving him a frightening glare. On the top of his arm, spreading across his shoulder, he had a tattoo of a large rose, with two swallows carrying scrolls that bore our names – Mum's, Frankie's and mine. His hair was black and shiny with grease, combed back, with greying sideburns, which reminded me of Grandpa in the Munsters.

In our camp, as in most other permanent camps, each plot had its own outside tap, toilet block and electric box with pay meter. Each morning, Frankie and I would roll two big, shiny churns over to the tap and fill them, before dragging them both back to the door. We would have to work as a team, because as each of the churns was as tall as me, once it had been filled, it was near impossible to move. Once we got them back, they would be put out by the step and as the day progressed, the water would be poured out into jugs and pans to be boiled for baths, cooking, hot drinks and laundry.

My father rarely used our indoor bathroom, having no patience to wait for the water pot to boil. At the crack of dawn, even in winter, he would make his way over to the tap with a towel round his bare shoulders. He would bend over and let the icy water run over his head as he wet the end of his razor before scraping the freezing blade across his face. I watched through the window every morning as he wallowed like a bear beneath the cold tap. One Saturday morning, I would have been about six years old, I decided that I too would have a shave. After my father had put his razor back I borrowed it, and in two short strokes I took off both my eyebrows – the only facial hair I had available – before coming proudly out of the bathroom to show off the results of my efforts. Frankie screamed and my mother made me spend the next week wearing two coloured plasters where my eyebrows should have been until eventually they began to grow back.

When our father was at home he went shirtless, though he always wore braces, even over his bare shoulders. When he went out he was always smart, in short-sleeved shirts, dark jumpers, and a Del Boy sheepskin coat. When he came home, if he'd made good money, he would be in a cheerful mood and would sit me on his lap in his armchair;

a big dark brown one with a stand-up ashtray next to it that reached the armrest. He would draw me pictures of dinosaurs with blood on their teeth and curly gecko-like tails.

Sometimes, when he came home late, he would stand in the doorway of the room Frankie and I shared and he would wake us up for a chat. We'd stumble sleepily through to the living room, as he made us hot tea and jammy toast. We'd sit, dunking our toast in our teacups, as he asked us all that we'd been doing while he was away.

He liked to play games and tricks on us. One Halloween, he stalked the outside of the trailer in his old overalls, a butcher-style apron and a cone hat made out of Sellotape and old Christmas paper covered in little Santas. He banged on our windows, scaring the living daylights out of us, roaring with laughter as we screamed our heads off.

But his good moods were sporadic and unpredictable and it took very little to make him lose his temper. In those early days it was mostly our mother who was the butt of his anger, though I was given a hiding when I misbehaved. He seldom dared to hit Frankie, though. If ever he did raise his hand to her, she would scream the place down, and he'd back away. She was far more like him than I was, and knew just how to play him.

Despite that, I always looked forward to him coming back from work, unless our mother had said 'wait till your father gets home'. She didn't threaten us unless she was at the end of her tether, but when she did she always followed through, and we knew we were in trouble.

I loved my father, and I wanted with all my heart to please him and make him proud of me. But even in those early days, when I was first walking and talking, somehow I already knew that I didn't match up. I would spot him from the corner of my eye as I played, looking at me with an expression of irritation and dislike.

His glare made my heart feel as though he had crushed it with a rock. I wasn't showing any sign of becoming the muscle-bound He-Man he so wanted me to be, and whatever special energy those gold gloves were meant to bestow, it seemed I was immune to it.

With my mother it was far simpler. I adored her. She never spoke down to us and she taught us to appreciate what we had. She never made me feel the way my father did, however; she was not a warm or affectionate person and there was an aspect to her that was distant and untouchable. Yet I loved spending time with my mother and saw her as magical. It seemed to me she inhabited another world to the rest of us. One I longed to be a part of.

Neither of my parents ever said they loved us. Words like those were seen as a sign of weakness. But I could tell by the look my mother sometimes gave me that she did indeed love me. Even if she had wanted to be more openly affectionate, a look was as much as she could have given me. Women were strictly forbidden from 'mollycoddling' boys in case they compromised the tough masculinity that was expected of Gypsy men.

The one time our mother did show us affection, of a sort, was when we were ill. Like most Gypsy women, she was not keen on the benefits of modern medicine; she had more faith in the practice of positive thought, mixed with a touch of denial, and the odd old-wives' remedy. Her methods were slapdash, to say the least. When I caught cold, I'd be made to lie on the couch, mint leaves up my nose and whatever sauce she had a lot of in the cupboard slapped all over my chest.

'Let's get that ball of snot out of you,' she'd say as she rummaged through the kitchen drawer. Then, for one verse of 'Puff the Magic Dragon' she would tap a wooden spoon across my chest to break up the phlegm.

By the time the cold had reached Frankie, the method would have changed. Frankie would be laid out on her front, with a different kind of sauce over her back, and the mint leaves would be threaded around her neck on a shoelace. The only thing that was always part of the process was the wooden spoon tap. She would lightly bounce the spoon off Frankie's shoulder blades like a xylophone.

When Frankie came out in warts all over her hands our mother was convinced it was the revenge of a toad Frankie had crushed when she leaped from the trailer steps a few days earlier. She sent us out with a small bucket to collect some slugs, one slug for each wart. Once we had brought them home she squeezed the juice from the base of each slug, rubbing the slimy excess against each wart, while Frankie squealed and retched. Once basted in slug juice, Frankie's hands were wrapped in old carrier bags, which were then taped in place.

The next day I leaped out of bed and dragged Frankie from the top bunk to see if our mother's magic had worked as she had promised. To our dismay Frankie's hands were exactly as they had been before. Our mother, baffled by the failure of her foolproof medicine, drove us down to the local phone box to call Granny Bettie to see if there was some part of the process she had missed. We waited in the car as she waved her arms and shouted down the receiver. After slamming it down she stormed back into the car and headed for the local supermarket where she bought several packs of bacon, all of which were to be wrapped around Frankie's hands overnight, and then buried in the garden the next morning. This was solemnly done, but after a week of eager anticipation the warts had not budged. If anything they'd got bigger. At which point, accepting that she was a terrible failure as a witch, our mother finally caved and took Frankie to the doctor.

3

Sisters Grim

Our social life, such as it was, revolved around weddings, funerals and family get-togethers. There will never be a race that can do a wedding or a funeral like the Gypsies. In the Romany world everyone really does know everyone else, and many are related, so they will turn out in their hundreds.

Invitations weren't sent out. Word simply spread and guests turned up. On the whole, Gypsies aren't religious (though many, like my father, stuck a 'born again' fish to their cars and lorries to improve their chances of appearing honest and getting work) but usually choose to marry in church because they can fit in more people than in a registry office and it makes a better backdrop for the wedding photographs.

Our mother hated most social events, largely because whenever we all went to one, my father would end up causing a brawl. She often refused to go, so our father would go alone to represent all of us, and Frankie and I would breathe a sigh of relief because we didn't enjoy them any more than she did.

But there was no getting out of the wedding of our Aunt Nancy and Uncle Matthew. Aunt Nancy was our mother's youngest sister, the image of Granny Bettie, with exactly the same temperament. She would sometimes baby-sit for us, and the minute our parents' backs were turned she ordered us about like slaves, demanding that we make her a sandwich. With a bag of crisps. And a tea. And a glass of Coke. And then another bag of crisps. She would eat continuously, then throw me and Frankie out in the cold to play.

At her wedding Frankie and our cousins Olive and Twizzel were the bridesmaids and, when the pageboy from Uncle Matthew's side of the family fell ill, I was thrust into the role at the last minute. The boy's outfit was half my size, so my mum and Granny Bettie had to pull together to squeeze me into his little navy sailor suit, complete with Donald Duck hat. For the whole day, rather than slipping away for my usual bug hunt and catnap, I had to join the girls (who were dressed like the Lullaby League) in throwing petals on the ground wherever our fat aunt stomped. We got our revenge for being made to look like Munchkins by making evil faces and V signs in all the photos, before we were all found out and given a good public spanking.

While we didn't care for Aunt Nancy at all, we loved our mother's older sister Aunt Minnie: a chain-smoking kleptomaniac who came over twice a week to take our mother, Frankie and me out on a day trip to the nearest decent shopping centre.

Aunt Minnie would exit her Ford Capri in an avalanche of smoke, ash and tumbling, floor-length, hand-me-down mink coat, which would get caught up in the sharp points of her red heels as she clicked along the tarmac towards our trailer door.

She'd tug the mass of her coat through the front door as she climbed in.

'Morning, my little robbers. Where's your mum?'

Our mother would call out from the bedroom, 'Red shoes no knickers Minnie, ain't you ever heard that saying?'

'Well who says I *am* wearing knickers,' Minnie would laugh.

She'd spark up another cigarette and crash down on the couch next to me. Her voice was almost always indistinct because of the fag hanging from her lips.

'Make your old aunt a cuppa coffee, my babe,' she'd say to Frankie.

Frankie and I called her Aunt Cruella. At twenty-one (a near spinster in Gypsy terms), she had gone on two dates with Jaybus, an Elvis lookalike from Birmingham, and on the third she had married him. Having borrowed his father's car and worn a good suit on each occasion, he had convinced Aunt Minnie that she had caught herself a millionaire and would be set for life. Unfortunately, Uncle Jaybus was in fact a socially inept rag-and-bone man with a voice like Goofy in the cartoons. Frankie and I loved him. And, despite the initial disappointment, so did Aunt Minnie.

Once she realised her husband was not going to be able to look after her in the manner she wished for, she set about finding her own means of support – choring or stealing. She would tell friends to let her know what they wanted and when she had got a big enough list together, off she would go on the prowl. Having only one child, Romaine, who was a couple of years younger than us, she appointed me and Frankie as her accomplices. On big jobs, she would sometimes stop by our uncle Alfie's to pick up our cousins, Olive and Twizzel. The two of them were a year apart, like me and Frankie, but unlike us they couldn't stand the sight of one another. From the moment they got into Aunt Minnie's car they would be slyly hitting one another and only the promise of McDonalds would shut them both up.

A trip with our aunt Minnie was always an adventure. While our mother was doing her weekly shop in the supermarket, Frankie and I would push Romaine's buggy behind Aunt Minnie, who would sweep into a shop, swish her mink about, and, in an accent reminiscent of Margaret Thatcher's, bellow for the nearest sales assistant.

As Aunt Minnie spoke to the assistant, she would 'browse' the shelves, picking up each item she wanted us to take, and giving it a shake before placing it back on the hanger. We would load the pram, and our pockets, while Aunt Minnie dragged a hefty pile off to the changing room, with the hapless assistant in tow.

She would re-emerge several minutes later.

'Did you find anything, Miss?' the assistant would ask.

'No,' Aunt Minnie would declare, as she swished her coat. 'It was all total rubbish.' And she would walk out, her nose in the air and leave the shop empty handed, but double her original size. If she was discovered, she would scream '*Shav*!' (run). Frankie would grab me by the arm, then, pushing Romaine's buggy like a battering ram through the main doors, we would charge out into the crowds. If we were all separated, we all knew to meet back at Aunt Minnie's car. Sometimes she overtook us, ramming people out of our path with her great fur-clad shoulders and screaming that the store detective on her tail was a maniac trying to kill her, in the hope that some gullible bystander might wrestle him to the ground.

Back at the car park, Aunt Minnie took off the fur and hurled it into the boot. With a cigarette hanging from her lips, she would squirm around in the driver's seat, peeling off her layers, which usually included around six tops, three pairs of slacks and an evening gown.

Once we all got home, Aunt Minnie would stay around long enough for a couple of coffees before carting her goods back to camp to sell for the best price. Since it was 100 per cent profit, she was able to sell for knock-down prices, and there was always a queue for her wares.

We loved our outings with Minnie, which were often hilarious and always an adventure. Far less fun were the outings to our father's loud and overbearing family. But our visits to them were inescapable. Twice a week we piled into the van and drove to the home of my father's older brother Tory.

Tory Manor, as it was known by all, was the most palatial home within a twenty-mile radius. Granddad Noah and Uncle Tory had bought it with the plan that, with their wives and Noah and Ivy's youngest son, Joseph, they could live there together. But after just three days Granddad, miserable in a home that didn't have wheels, refused to live in it any longer.

He set up home with Granny Ivy, their fifteen-year-old Jack Russell, Sparky, and Uncle Joseph in a brand-new, thirty-five-foot, bright pink Winnebago-style caravan at the top of the paddock behind the main house. This was their dream home, and they spared nothing on the decor. A swarm of fake butterflies the size of cats were nailed along the walls, a giant dust ruffle built entirely out of curved bright red bricks surrounded the caravan's base, and each of its two entrances spewed steps that twirled like helter-skelters to the ground. The paddock was resurfaced, and given a separate entrance off the road that led up to the main house, so that Granddad Noah could keep his prized Rolls-Royce within a few feet of the living-room window.

Once they had settled in, Granddad Noah and Granny Ivy were delighted, as were Uncle Tory and his family, who got the main house to themselves.

The caravan was Granny Ivy's pride and joy and she liked to keep it immaculate. But as she was so small she was unable to reach most of the table-tops in her new home, she had her sister Tiny over to help out with the daily chores. Our Aunt Tiny shared the same throaty cackle, penchant for gold teeth and love of fur-trimmed moccasins as her sister. But in all other respects they were utterly different. Tiny stood as tall and broad as a wardrobe and could have used Granny Ivy as a hand puppet. As well as the moccasins, she wore a pink floral pinny that she never took off. It had two large pockets that draped just below her huge and low-slung breasts; one for her yellow rubber gloves, and the other for her cigarettes and solid gold lighter in the shape of a horse's head.

Aunt Tiny had given up on the 'Gypsy woman of a certain age' black hair-dye regime. Instead she bore a large white curly Afro, which made her look like a circus clown. Every day she would arrive at the caravan and whiz around, duster in her yellow-gloved hand, scrubbing everything from waist-height upward, while Granny Ivy did everything below.

Unfortunately for Granny Ivy, her end of the deal also

meant washing the dog. Sparky had been bought by Noah as an anniversary present for her, but sadly the two developed an instant mutual hatred. Sparky spent every day lying in the darkness underneath the couch, waiting for Ivy to pass by so that he could jump out and bite her on the backside. To add to his annoyance, for the past three years he had been unable to poo without the aid of Joseph and a rubber glove. With Joseph being the only family member willing to do such a chore, the old dog had warmed to him and would scarcely leave his side.

Although the great house was just yards away, the whole family would always gather in the pink caravan every Friday evening, when Granddad and Uncle Tory would host a cock-fighting tournament out in the vast gardens. Each week several cockerels would fight to the death . . . or until Granddad Noah put the loser out of its misery by decapitating it with the end of a shovel.

Uncle Tory's wife, Aunt Maudie, who lived in pink-velour tracksuits, see-through high heels and had enormous fake breasts, would sooner have dropped dead than have the 'riff-raff' that came along to these fights set foot inside her home, so she made us kids – Frankie and me, Tory and Noah and their twin sisters Donna and Carlene – gather twigs and set up a camp fire that would keep the men warm and well away from her house until the party was over. Our reward was the marshmallows she would give us to cook over the fire.

Although Donna and Carlene were a year younger than me, they were both twice my size. The Walsh clan commented constantly that Frankie and the girls looked like triplets, and they did, but in truth, this owed less to genetics than to the fact that, much to our mother's annoyance, Aunt Maudie was a serial copycat, and her two girls were given exactly the same hairstyles and clothes as Frankie.

There was always a rowdy crowd, most of whom were fellow trainers from the boxing club up the road where Uncle Tory spent a lot of his time. Some of the visitors would bring their own cockerels, but the majority just came along to watch. All of the men would make bets, which would all be handled by Uncle Tory, who also charged a joining fee to make a bit of extra profit.

Most of the fighting birds were caged in home-made hutches, strapped down into the rear of the lorries. My uncle Duffy (like most of our 'uncles', not an uncle at all) kept his in a boarded-up dog kennel on the back of his Ford pick-up. One week he arrived with a new cockerel named Red. It was as big as a chair, with a sharpened beak, which Uncle Duffy had filed down himself, and not one feather on his body. When Uncle Duffy opened that passenger door, we kids ran for our lives, for fear his pterodactyl of a cockerel would peck our eyes out.

After several weeks as reigning champion, we watched old Red get torn apart by a sneaky, fully feathered newcomer. Frankie, the twins and I huddled on top of the old well watching, as the two birds clucked, hissed, pecked and sprayed blood all over the lawn.

I could never erase the guilt I felt for not jumping in and trying to save the losing chicken. Often, unable to stand the suffering any more, we kids would go into the house to watch *Loony Tunes* on TV. But as old Red fought his last, none of us could move. The twins covered their eyes as Frankie stared, transfixed but still chomping away, her hand dipping in and out of her bag of marshmallows.

It wasn't long before the younger bird finally pecked through old Red's neck and he had to face the final relief of Granddad Noah's shovel. There was a loud cheer and the passing of money among the men as Old Noah gathered up Red on the spoon of the shovel and tossed him into the fire.

Frankie put down her marshmallows and walked over to the flames. She wanted to see the bird close up for the first and last time without running away in terror. But as she stepped up to the fire, the great chicken's flaming corpse leaped from it with a wild scream. We children shouted in terror and the crowd ran in all directions as the bird, its head hanging by a thread, darted across the garden in a crazy dance of death. Only the men – my father, Uncle Tory, Old Noah and a few of the others – laughed their heads off, as the rest of us scattered.

In a bid to escape the madness of the cock fights and the pink trailer, I would often wander off alone into the extensive grounds of Tory Manor. Scattered among them were giant flowers, curved willows, ivory-barked trees and a set of curious stone dancers, each frozen in a wonderful gesture. Over time, many of them had been swallowed up in the heavy foliage, and others had been disfigured or decapitated by one of young Tory or Noah's hunting weapons. As well as their Samurai swords, catapults and pellet guns, the boys had a harpoon gun, which they fired into trees, statues, and even unsuspecting pigeons. I'd had a go once, but misfired, getting the teeth of the harpoon trapped three inches below the surface of a tree root just inches from my toes.

Like my mother, I was at my happiest alone. And in the vast grounds of Tory Manor I could sing to myself at the top of my lungs without being heard, and make believe that this land was my kingdom.

Beyond the rotting tennis court and the chicken-fighting arena was a hedgerow maze with a Koi pond at its heart. The sound of the fountain that sprang from the pond would beckon as I wound my way through the maze. Above the fountain a white marble mermaid sat on a rock, reaching out to all those who had made it around the final corner of the maze. The paving that surrounded her home was damp and furry with moss and I would sit cross-legged by the side and watch, fascinated as the great golden fish in the pond appeared just beneath the surface.

Granddad Noah loved a get-together even more than most Gypsies, and would find any old excuse to invite family and friends to the pink trailer. Most Sundays we gathered there for Sunday dinner.

Inside the trailer the lounge was a shrine to the family and its achievements. Family portraits and celebrity-signed boxing gloves hung in every spare gap on the pale walls, while trophies won by my father and Uncle Tory were dotted among the Crown Derby plates, teapots and china cups that were displayed on every shelf.

The bright red leather three-piece suite was festooned with yards of home-made lace, and six crystal vases, that stood a good foot taller than Granny Ivy, were lined up across the window shelf like a regiment of jewelled cannons.

Granny Ivy's spot was a central, throne-like chair, made especially for her. It had huge armrests and a footstool to help her climb up into the high cushioned seat that put her at the same height as everyone else. Next to her chair, a tiny arm's reach away, was her breathing machine; a torpedo of green copper, with a motor-bike engine, a long pipe and a gas mask, which she would attach to her face at regular intervals.

My father and Granddad Noah would always take the two lace-covered armchairs that faced the TV, while the other men perched on the sofa or around the room. Aunt Tiny, Aunt Prissy, my mother and any other wives would sit the other end of the room around the dining table and Granny Ivy would serve up either her '90 per cent turnip' roast or a traditional Gypsy favourite known as Jimmy Grey, which consisted of swede, onions, animal fat, liver, beefsteak, chicken and pork, all shallow fried and served up with a heavily buttered crusty loaf, with a ladle of the leftover dripping from the tray to dip it in.

Guests would outdo themselves in telling far-fetched stories, while Granny Ivy, Joseph, Granddad Noah and my father would all take turns passing out cold. Sometimes they all fell asleep together in mid-conversation, having bored each other to sleep. Our mother and Aunt Prissy would be left to say the goodbyes to any other guests and help Aunt Tiny clean up the mess. After which they would empty their make-up bags and rummage through closets for anything we kids could use to give our sleeping victims a full makeover.

Granny Ivy, being a woman, was never as fun to make-up and Joseph's place next to the dreaded Sparky always got him off lightly. So every week, either our father or

Granddad Noah would wake up to find themselves wearing Minnie Mouse ears and a full face of slap.

In between the food, the stories, the re-runs of matinee westerns and trying not to stare as Joseph, an ugly, moody mountain of a man, gorged himself on packets of raw bacon, Frankie and I would be asked to get up and sing for the family.

It was a tradition at any Gypsy gathering for those present to sing a song, and everyone had their own personal favourite, ready for the moment when they were asked to get up. Matthew Docherty or Slim Whitman tracks were most popular among the men, and a party was never complete without at least five women knocking out a pitch-perfect Patsy Cline hit. Granddad Noah sometimes paid me and Frankie a pound to sing, simply to save everyone from yet another rendition of 'Honky Tonk Angels' or 'Crazy'.

Frankie's regular solo was a Gypsy song, 'Blackbird, I Av'ee', which always went down well, and mine was a Dean Martin number, 'Ol' Scotch Hat', a song that I had learned from our mother.

Our mother's voice was a phenomenal instrument. She was able to mimic any great singer she chose. People always asked her to do Patsy Cline, because she did it so well, but she could also knock out a brilliant Nancy Sinatra, doing 'These Boots Are Made for Walking' and many country favourites. She was pestered endlessly to sing at parties.

Frankie and I would finish the party with 'Show Me the Way to Go Home', by which point it was always past midnight and tired children and merry adults would pile into cars and trucks.

These visits to Tory Manor and the pink trailer were the social highlight of our week. We seldom went on family outings, although from time to time our father took us to the local safari park. He would make all of us get under a blanket in the back of his lorry, then say at the kiosk that he was working on the grounds and they'd wave him in. Once inside we'd climb into the front and Frankie and I would point excitedly at the animals.

In the summer we would all meet at Uncle Tory's house and then drive in convoy down to the seaside where we spent the whole day. The men and the children swam, while the women sat, fully clothed, on the beach, gossiping and smoking. It wasn't considered decent for them to strip off.

Unlike the others, I was afraid of the sea. I couldn't go near it without the theme tune of the film *Jaws* popping into my head. The horrific image of the great shark eating people alive had lodged in my head when our father sat us in front of the film and I was never able to forget it. So instead of swimming I spent hours looking around the rocks for crabs, which I would bring home and keep in a bucket on the doorstep.

But the most exciting time of year was Christmas. At that time of year my father would pursue another of his sidelines: flogging Christmas trees and wreaths at Borough Market in London.

Frankie, our mother and I would sit at the kitchen table making hundreds of festive wreaths out of twigs, holly leaves and fake snow spray. We would spend whole days working there, so that a stack of the wreaths would be ready for our father to collect them when he came home.

It was my fourth Christmas, when an earthquake throughout the trailer at 5 a.m. turned out to be our mother. She was as excited as a child, unable to wait a second longer. She rattled at the sides of the bunk beds.

'Get up, you herbs, it's Christmas! He's been. Quick, go and look!'

We ran into the lounge, which had been covered with balloons and tinsel, diving into the pile of presents, screaming out for joy.

After much digging, I couldn't help but notice that every single one was labelled with Frankie's name. I felt as if I was going to vomit from disappointment.

'I think he forgot me, Mum.'

My father took me in his arms and pointed through the window.

There, in the navy blue of 5 a.m. stood a brand-new bright red, big-wheeled, battery-operated quad bike, complete with shiny leather-bound boxing gloves that dangled from the handlebars like a bull's testicles.

Mum grabbed her camera as we all made our way outside.

'Get on it then,' cried my father, with a joyful prod to my chest.

I eyed the monster cautiously, intimidated, by the testosterone that was seeping from every shiny inch of it. Hesitating, I stood beside it, flicking at the boxing gloves and sending them whirling around the handlebars.

Frankie marched over and gave me a boot up onto the driver seat. 'Just press on that peddle and it'll go,' boomed my father.

I was terrified of the thing. I sat cautiously on it, and

placed my foot on the pedal, looking back at the three of them. My father's face was beaming through the dark like a lantern. Then, desperate to please him but with no idea of what I was doing, I slammed down on the accelerator. After eight feet I crashed the monster into a wall, bouncing off to mangle a neighbour's fence, before flying through the air into a patch of Busy Lizzies.

I could hear my father's groans as I pulled myself from the dirt patch, battered and bruised. I scraped the mud from my pyjamas and slunk back inside, leaving the ugly death machine and its gloves where they had crashed.

I was hot with shame, knowing I was not like other boys, who made their fathers proud. I was a failure, and I couldn't look at my dad's face.

By the time I got back indoors, my sister had already clawed her way through her first present: a baby doll nearly twice the size of her, bald as a coot, and wearing a tea-stained Babygro. She flicked the switch at the back of its head and it began to wail disturbingly, rolling its head around like the girl from *The Exorcist*.

'I'm gonna call him Jesus,' she chirped, ramming a dummy into the beast's mouth.

She put Jesus down to rip open another present and I ran over to help her control the thing as it began vibrating its way across the floor.

'You don't like the bike then?' groaned my father. 'You ain't getting nothing else, you know.'

'It's all right, I'll play on it tomorrow,' I said, looking down at my feet.

I was sure as hell never going to sit on that death trap again.

Two days later, it was gone. I was relieved, and Frankie was glad to share the parenting of Jesus with me.

The handlebar gloves, though, were not: they had been hung from the corner of my bed, a symbol of what was to come.

4

Taking a Punch

By the time I was four my grooming process had begun. My father was now working locally and, having found a regular grunter, was home a lot more often, so he had plenty of free time between watching the soap operas both he and my mother loved to dedicate to training his only son.

Before he began he beckoned me over to the battered easy chair which was his throne and lifted the golden gloves from around my neck. 'You need to show me how worthy you are of wearing these, my boy, all right?' he said, tugging the chain over his own head.

Although the eventual aim was bare-knuckle, the training was done with boxing gloves on, as the moves were basically the same. My father pulled his treasured, ancient brown leather gloves over his sandpaper hands, making a few mock punches, to gear himself up. 'Right, you ready?'

My own small gloves had been taken from the end of my bed and tied on around my wrists. 'Yep.'

He told me to stand with my arms in the air. Then he punched me in the ribs. A small punch, at first, just enough to startle me, and hurt a bit. Then another, and another, each one harder, so that by the third I was winded and by the fifth I was doubled over in agony.

This was my first lesson, he said, laughing. How to take

a punch. The rules, which he explained as I clutched my aching ribs, were that I had to take at least ten levels of blow, without crying, bobbing, weaving or dodging. 'In at the deep end', was his approach. He had learned that from his father, Old Noah, who used to say 'bring your boy up like a wolf, and a wolf you will get'.

But for my father it was more than just the harsh tuition he'd had himself. He seemed to need to test his own strength, in case he may have weakened since the days when he fought and won against all comers. He didn't hold back, when he hit me.

That session, like all those that were to follow, ended with 'real' punches, tears and at least thirty minutes of my father raving about how ashamed of me he was, how I was a pathetic coward and he didn't know how he'd ever make a man of me.

I tried. I tried really hard. But the blows hurt so much. Taking them without crying was more than I could manage. In every session, by the third or fourth blow, my small body shuddered with pain and I collapsed in tears. I knew what that meant, so I would be sure to collapse into the tightest ball that I possibly could.

'You're (punch) nothing! (punch-punch) Nothing but a cowardly (punch-kick) piece of (punch) shit!'

Soon I dreaded the 'training' so much that I began kicking up an almighty fuss when he announced it was time. But it didn't matter whether I kicked, screamed, pleaded or begged, I had to do it. Every single day. Punches, followed by harder punches, fury and humiliation.

And every day I failed him.

As the training sessions went on, I found it impossible

to sit in the lounge and watch telly with him there. I couldn't stop staring at him, watching as he skipped from channel to channel. I felt an axe was dangling over my head. And once he put down that remote control I knew it was time.

'Ready, Mikey?'

I was never ready, and I was never less than terrified.

I was not yet old enough to go to school, and I was expected to take hit after hit from a grown man, get off my backside when I fell, and come back fighting.

Almost all Gypsy men are violent, it's ingrained in the culture and the life they lead and impossible to avoid. My father had no doubt suffered as a child, and because of Old Noah and his motto, he grew up to be more violent than most.

The 'great' name we were burdened with was a guarantee that violence would seek us out. My father knew that there would always be a new challenger. Leagues of men held grudges for his victories, and the sons of those he had beaten were waiting in the wings. Waiting to fight me and claim their place amongst the ranks of the victors.

My father wanted me to be ready, and if beating the life out of me was the only way to toughen and prepare me for that day, then so be it.

My mother watched our daily fight, tight-lipped. She had known my fate before I was even born. She knew about the family she had married into, and what the men were like. But what she hadn't known was how it would feel to see her child being attacked unmercifully, time after time, and forced to play a 'game' which he could never win, leaving him a bruised, battered, weeping heap on the floor.

On one occasion Frankie was roped in to count the punches.

'Punch number three, you ready?' I swallowed and nodded squeezing my eyes shut. 'You keeping count, my gal?'

'Yep,' clucked Frankie, her back to the action, squirming to keep Jesus from leaping out of her grip.

I closed my eyes, tensing my whole body, awaiting the next blow. I dived into my unconscious, searching frantically for a place to hide myself from what was coming.

WHAM!

Like a wrecking ball, his fist crashed into my guts and sent me hurtling across the floor.

I tripped backward over my mother, who was lying on the floor, engrossed in a re-run of *Starsky and Hutch*. I crash-landed into the television set, pushing it off the stand. My mother got up and peeled me from the telly. 'That's enough now, Frank.' Her voice was tight and low.

My father chuckled, rearranged his boxing gloves, and ignored her. 'Get up then, boy,' he ordered.

But my mother, nerves frayed by having to listen to my gasps and sobs, wasn't giving up. 'Haven't you had enough tonight?' she asked him.

Whimpering, I climbed to my feet, rubbing my throbbing ribs with the boxing gloves, which, by that time, had cut off my circulation.

'Ready?'

He leaned forward from his easy chair, hissing and sparring with himself, waiting for me to come back for the next punch.

My mother grew more agitated.

'Oi, pig's head! I've said that's enough! Now sit back in your fucking throne before you break it.'

'Shut your fucking mouth, and watch your murder mystery,' he hissed. 'Come on then, Mikey.'

I hesitated.

'I'm gonna count to three . . . one . . .'

'Dad, please.'

'Two . . .'

I turned to run, getting one step before being lifted from the floor with an almighty kick. As I fell, he ripped off a glove and dragged me in towards him.

Suddenly, in a graceful leap from the carpet, my mother snatched me from his clutches, punching him square on the nose.

My father rose from his throne, grabbing her by the hair.

Leaping onto him, she pushed her fingers into his eyes and nudged me out of the firing line with her foot.

'Run, Mikey, run.'

Frankie threw Jesus to the floor, and rushed to my aid, pulling me up. Without looking back we stumbled down the hallway and into the bedroom.

'Come back here, boy, I haven't finished with you yet!'

Frankie slammed the door shut, fumbling frantically with the bolt as our mother rushed to stand in front of it.

We held onto each other, screaming, as our mother was chased and ripped from the doorframe.

'Don't open that door,' my mother screeched.

Backing into the corner we listened to him dragging her from the door, and then wails followed by thuds, thuds followed by wails and the vibrations of bodies slamming against walls, appliances and cupboards.

Then silence.

A moment later we heard footsteps coming toward the door. Our father's.

'Unlock this door. Now.'

We didn't dare disobey.

Our mother, sprawled on the kitchen floor, unconscious, was deaf to my cries as I was dragged back into the lounge, with Frankie hanging onto my feet.

Now launched on a violent rampage, his wrath unsuppressed, my father was going to finish the job and reaffirm his position as master of the house.

I was thoroughly beaten and we were sent back to our room. We stopped beside our mother, and Frankie tried to lift her face from a pile of broken china.

'Don't touch her!'

We backed away from her prostrate body and ran back down the hall and into the bedroom. We heard the telly come back on and knew he was watching it.

We sat on the floor, both of us terrified and whimpering. Was our mother dead? We didn't know. We wanted to go to her, but we didn't dare.

It must have been half an hour later that we heard the chink of the broken crockery being cleared away. We looked at one another, both thinking the same thing. Did that mean she was all right?

Slowly, without making a sound, Frankie opened the door, just a crack. Enough to see that our mother was on her feet, in the kitchen.

'She's OK,' Frankie whispered.

Relief flooded through me. If she had died, I knew it would have been my fault.

The pattern was set that day: my daily training, in between the soaps, with our mother intervening when she thought I'd had enough and Frankie and I running off to the bedroom until the storm was over.

Our mother was always a very 'dust yourself off and move on' kind of woman.

She constantly made excuses for our father, to avoid any gossip. The dark staining of her front teeth, she claimed, was caused by me hitting her with a spoon when I was a baby. But everyone knew that it was not a spoon, but our father ramming her face into the side of a sink bowl, also breaking her cheek bone. This was yet another night after training, the same night my nose was broken by a punch from my father, for crying.

I still have images of the awful things he would do to my mother as punishment for stepping in to try to protect me. She was regularly thrown to the floor, stamped on, held down and punched, while her hair was torn out in clumps from her head. But she would take it all, never making a sound, never crying in front of him, and never giving in.

She didn't seem to hold it against him, either. Despite these horrors, our parents were still affectionate with one another. My father would kiss my mother and give her a bear hug whenever he came home. She, in turn, would often come up from the floor where she was lying in front of the TV to sit on his lap. He would call Frankie to join her and then proudly brag of his girls as he lifted them up and down like trophies.

The other Gypsies who lived around us were aware of my father's violence; no one could have missed the thuds and crashes that echoed from our trailer daily. But they were all far too frightened of him to do anything about it. Even if they had, my mother would not have accepted it. She knew him better than anyone. She fought her own battles and got him back, by never letting him win. He might knock her out, but that didn't mean she had surrendered.

She fought him hard, and courageously. But in time, the beatings took effect, and she gradually got the confidence and spirit she once had knocked right out of her, so that by the time I was almost five, it was she who had fallen into silence.

Many women outside the situation she was in would have walked away, never to come back. But she was a Gypsy wife, and to leave would have meant becoming an outcast. So she covered up and excused her husband for the cruel way he treated her, and she found refuge in us, and in music.

Sometimes work would take our father away for weeks on end; at others he would spend whole days sitting in front of the telly, putting me through the training routine two or three times a day. Luckily for me he had a fairly active social life when he was home and would often disappear to the local betting office or the pub.

When he was away, everything changed, and the three of us had fun. We would record ourselves on Mum's old stack music system, singing karaoke at the top of our lungs. Our party piece was from her favourite Barbara Streisand album, and at five I learned the Donna Summer part to 'Enough is Enough' which my mother and I would belt out together, while Frankie did a manic kind of rain dance around the trailer.

Mum introduced us to Michael Jackson, who would be blasted throughout the camp from our speakers as we sang along to 'Thriller', Frankie doing Michael and me roaring the monster sounds and miming the Vincent Price bit. We practically wore out the tape of the music video, which our mother had bought for us, joyously watching over and over again, practising the dance moves and debating which zombie was the coolest and prettiest.

We weren't bothered by the zombies at all, since we watched our father's grizzly collection of horror movies on a regular basis and had by now seen much worse. He would get hold of bootleg copies of banned films, and make us watch them, as one of his more minor forms of punishment, so aged four I sat in front of *The Texas Chainsaw Massacre*, *The Evil Dead* and *Child's Play*. They scared us dreadfully; I often had nightmares and Jesus would be locked firmly away at nights in case he came to life and searched in the cupboards for kitchen knives to wield against us.

We loved TV, and were avid fans of *The Muppet Show*. As a sixth birthday surprise for Frankie, our mother's brother Alfie, a 400-pound giant, dressed up as what he thought was Miss Piggy. He woke us up in the middle of the night, squealing at the top of his voice. Our shrieks of horror were louder, though. We thought this horrific apparition in the doorway was the *Texas Chainsaw* murderer Leatherface, coming to kill us.

The films we loved to watch arrived courtesy of Big Jabba John, the only Gypsy man in the south of England who could get a video tape of any movie you asked for within days of request. He spent most of his time either ripping off rentals in his trailer, or sitting in the front row of a cinema with an almost steady video camera. Every Monday night, he would arrive in our camp in his rumbling beast of a pick-up, the back full to the brim with cassette tapes and video boxes. As soon as we heard the roar of its exhaust as it hit the gateway ramp, every man, woman and child came running from their caravans, screaming and waving their hands in the air. By the time he left, Frankie and I would be starting a Disney movie marathon, over fish and chips, sticky buns, Angel Delight and toffee popcorn.

While our father bagged yet another horror film, our mother preferred epic love stories, which sent me and Frankie into comas on the carpet in front of the TV. Frankie would eventually drag me out and we would flee from the trailer into the garden. It was while escaping a weepy Liz Taylor movie that Frankie leaped from the trailer door, right onto the jagged edge of a broken milk bottle. Our father rushed her off to hospital, where she was given thirteen stitches in the bottom of her foot.

No matter what movie we watched, our father was always fast asleep within fifteen minutes, or at the point when he had eaten all that was left of the snacks, whichever came first. We got wise to it, hiding away half the sweets until he was out cold and snoring like a warthog, when we'd bring them out and munch away through the rest of the film.

Our mother had been waiting a long time for Big Jabba John to get her a copy of her favourite movie, promising us that we'd love it when we saw it. When he finally delivered, Frankie and I couldn't wait. We were hoping for something along the lines of *Jaws*, but our mother assured us it was nothing of the sort. She giggled with delight as she put it in the video recorder, calling over her shoulder, 'Mikey, go and get the box of Maltesers out of the cupboard.'

We pulled the blinds and spread ourselves out around the living room. Frankie, in a sulk because it wasn't *Jaws*, stretched herself across the couch, so I took my place on the floor, sharing mother's cushion and making sure I was within reach of the Malteser box.

Our mother had finally made a good choice; the film was *The Wizard of Oz* and it enchanted us. After that Frankie and I began a ritual of watching it daily, then going out into the garden to act out our favourite moments from it. Frankie was always the wicked witch, while I was her faithful, flying monkey. Together we would swing back and forth on an old rope that our father had tied to a tree branch, flying through the air before taking a great cackle-filled leap to the ground.

Our tree was divided into two halves, separated by a rickety wooden fence. Beyond it was the backyard of our Gorgia neighbours, who had three daughters, all around our age, with white-blond hair in plaits and matching red raincoats.

We were always conscious of them watching us through the gaps in the trees, but were warned not to ever speak to them. 'Gorgia-breds,' our mother would say. 'Don't you ever speak to them, even if they talk to you. They'll have you taken away.'

The prejudice went both ways. 'Come away from there,' we'd hear their mother say as she shoved them back into the house. 'They're Gypsies, and they'll put a curse on you.'

One day Frankie and I heard the girls whispering. 'Gypsies, look it's the Gypsies.'

Frankie, ignoring our mother's advice, began swearing at them.

'Yucky yucky Gypsies, yucky yucky Gypsies,' the girls began to chant.

Our father had given us a whole directory of obscenities to work with so we were streets ahead in this particular contest.

'Whores, go fuck yourself!' Frankie shouted.

While the three huddled to debate whether Frankie's strange words were a Gypsy curse, she put a cupped hand to my ear and told me what to say.

'And eat some dog shit!' I squeaked.

At this point the girls' furious parents emerged from the bushes. Frankie and I ran into the trailer, slamming the door of our bedroom as we lay in wait for the parents to come over and complain. But they didn't dare set foot in the camp, and we never saw the girls at the fence again.

We had no idea of the meaning of the words we used, but it was not uncommon for Gypsy children to be subjected to, and encouraged to use, swear words and we regarded them as just another part of our vocabulary.

A few weeks after our encounter with the girls over the fence, a fire broke out in our trailer. The old portable heater we used had been left on in the front room, and Frankie had left her teddy bear next to it.

Frankie and I were fast asleep when our mother ran into our room and shook us awake then ripped us from our beds and threw us at my father, who was outside the bedroom door. Peering over my father's shoulder, terrified and fascinated, I saw flames and flying pieces of burning fabric everywhere. As he ran outside with us, black smoke billowed down the hall, the whole lounge was engulfed in flames and the trailer began to tilt.

As our home went up in smoke, we went over to my father's cousin Dwayne's trailer to wait for the fire brigade. By the time they arrived everything had gone, and all that was left was the chassis the trailer had rested on.

Our parents were philosophical – trailer fires weren't unusual – and the next day my father set about getting us a new trailer. He wouldn't have been insured, but his family all helped, and a new trailer was duly bought and installed in the same spot. Inside it was almost identical to the first, but there were few survivors from our toys. Jesus had somehow escaped with nothing worse than a hideous head burn, but the Cabbage Patch army had been reduced to black smudges on the concrete. Despite this, Frankie and I thought the fire was exciting, and we played fire engines for weeks afterwards.

One evening my father came home boasting about having just gatecrashed Diana Dors' funeral. Apparently, he and his friend Matthew, driving further afield than usual in the search for work, had stopped for a few drinks and then stumbled upon the event, and had followed the line of black limousines as they entered the churchyard. I can picture the crowd of mourners, paying their final respects to Britain's Blonde Bombshell, as a couple of drunken Gypsies watched, sprawled against a pick-up truck in their bright green overalls, clashing beer cans, hooting, jeering and pointing out the celebrities.

My father and his brothers loved to brag about rubbing shoulders with stars. Diana Dors' funeral became a morbid tit-bit for my father to boast about. While my Uncle Tory bragged non-stop about the 'stars' he rubbed shoulders with through the boxing club he frequented, my father and Uncle Matthew sought out celebrities for odd jobs, sometimes successfully. One of my father's favourite anecdotes was cutting down a tree for Cliff Richard, then scaring him half to death a year later by jumping out at him from behind a lorry, shouting 'Oi, Cuntsmouth'.

Most of what my father got up to was illegal. And even the jobs he did legally were often botched, so it was inevitable that the law would catch up with him. One day, our mother leaped into the trailer, looking terrified.

'Frankie, they've come for you. The wardrobe, quick.'

Half asleep after putting me through my rounds, my father dived from his armchair and tumbled to the floor, then sped towards the bedroom.

'Shit! His arse print's still in the chair,' screamed Frankie, jumping up and down on the crater in his seat.

My mother grabbed her, and with one of us under each arm, charged through the hall and slung us into the bedroom behind him like a couple of trash bags.

Our father was stuffing himself inside the closet, throwing old clothes and toys over himself as a disguise. 'Shut the wardrobe, Mikey.'

I charged over, pulling the door across, as he hissed, 'Say one word, my boy, and I'll kill you.'

Frankie leaped onto a stool and pressed her face against the window.

'Get down from there you fool,' cried my mother, slapping make-up across her face for a five-second 'everything is fine officer' makeover.

'MUUUUM! I wanna see 'em!' Frankie bawled.

As my mother dragged her off the stool, there were three loud bangs on the front door.

'What do they want?' I whispered

'They've come to take your dad away, so, whatever you do, shut up.'

Mother answered the door while Frankie got back up on the stool by the window and I climbed under the bed. I didn't want to look at the police for fear of giving my father's presence away.

From my hiding place I stared at the wardrobe.

One little word might stop him ever hurting me again. Just one word. But I was too scared. If he wasn't taken away, he would kill me.

He got away with it that time. But by the time I reached my fifth Christmas, my father was finally caught, and we were shifted into a bungalow, owned by our granddad Alfie, while he went to prison.

5

A Bungalow with Barbie Graveyard

We didn't miss life in a caravan. In the bungalow we now had heat, doors with sturdy locks, bigger rooms and our own garden to play in.

Our mother loved being able to do up her new home. In the trailers she'd lived in, most of the decor was already fitted and there wasn't much scope for adding her own touches. She hated the traditional Gypsy women's 'home and garden' look; all Crown Derby, with an abundance of brass Shire-horse ornaments and masses of garish china everywhere. Now, with a real house, a budget and no husband to tell her what to do, she was free to let rip with her own taste – which we discovered, after only a few days, was not too dissimilar to that of Elton John.

Every time Frankie and I came in from the garden there would be a new and even more elaborate piece of furnishing that she had just finished. Layer upon layer of pastel ruffles soon hung from each window frame, and after a couple of trips to the garden centre we found ourselves surrounded by a whole troop of creamy Roman statues bearing bunches of lilacs.

Throughout the months that my father was in prison, our mother spun around the house, living out a series of Doris Day decorating moments. She was always painting something or redecorating something and she loved to explain what she was doing as she worked. Frankie and I were happy to be her audience. We would sit, Frankie holding Jesus, me with my new favourite, Skeletor, as she hammered, tore up and painted, while describing, just like someone on a TV makeover show, exactly what she was doing with a yard of cream curtain, some gold paint and a bag of fake flowers.

With our father gone there was peace and harmony in the home. Our mother was never violent towards us, we had fun with her, and with the fear of my father removed I was at my happiest.

When we tired of watching her decorate, Frankie and I spent most of our days out in the garden making recipes from mud, eggs, Play-Doh, canned meat and captured spiders. We made up for our lack of a pool by taking turns sitting in a tin bucket filled with water, and we constructed our own bird traps for the swarms of crows that regularly haunted the place, hoping to keep one of them and teaching it how to speak. Of course we never managed to get hold of one, but as a consolation prize, we did stumble across the occasional crow corpse, which we solemnly buried, complete with eulogy and coffin.

By the time we had been in the bungalow for a couple of months our graveyard had a population of four crows, one flattened toad, what we thought might have been a mouse and Frankie's most vile and disposable Barbie Doll.

'Old Red Legs ... too ugly to live' was her eulogy: abrupt, brief and straight to the point. She was lucky to have had one at all. Old Red Legs was born with a defect that sealed her fate; her wondrous pins, though beautiful in shape, were (through the fault of her maker) as red as pigs' blood, which made her an embarrassment in mini-dresses, and according to my sister 'a psycho'. So it was no surprise that she was eventually found dead by Barbie and Co., naked, shaven-headed and hideously deformed, having been ravaged by a stray dog.

The heavy influence of horror movies may have played a significant part in our behaviour. That, and the ridiculous number of funerals we were made to attend, most of them for relatives we had never heard of.

Gypsy funerals tend to bring out every person who even passed the time of day with the deceased, and there were never less than 500 people there. Cars and lorries would be stacked with wreaths, and mourners would gather around a huge coffin, filled with belongings and garish jewellery for the dead person to take with them to the after-life. Not many Gypsies actually believe in an after-life any more, but the traditions have outlasted the beliefs. Some of the coffins we saw as children were so stacked with ornaments, jewels and even cartons of cigarettes that the undertakers must have had to sit on the lid of the coffin just to get the thing closed.

Not only did we children have to go along, but we were also forced to kiss the corpse goodbye. A chair would be pulled over, so that I could lean reluctantly over the edge of the coffin of some crone who had already been dead for a couple of weeks, and with a solemn 'goodbye' to the deceased, plant a kiss on the ice-cold forehead. The only way I could bear it was to screw my eyes tight shut.

Aunt Cissy, Granddad Noah's aunt, had lived to be a hundred because, it was rumoured, she had sold her soul to a strange creature that lived under a bridge. Aunt Cissy was the living image of the witch from *Snow White*; and ironically, she used to give us an apple for Christmases and birthdays, stuffed with a fifty-pence piece for good luck.

She was frightening enough to gaze upon when she was alive, but knowing that we would have to kiss her dead face at her funeral was terrifying. Frankie and I did our best to escape, but were dragged back and lifted onto the chair by her coffin together.

We stared, transfixed, at her painted orange face and purple lipstick, surrounded by sausage-shaped ringlets, put around her face to 'pretty her up'. I went in first, squeezing my eyes tight shut and leaning in. When my lips touched her forehead, I was afraid they were going to stick – her skin felt like that of a frozen turkey. Frankie went next and she couldn't have looked more horrified if she'd been asked to eat dog shit.

Our mother would regularly take us to visit her parents, Granny Bettie and Granddad Alfie. Our father never came with us because he and Granny Bettie hated the sight of one another. Granny Bettie was an expert at insults and put-downs and she saved her worst for our father. On the rare occasions when they met, they sparred like prize-fighters and, to everyone's surprise, it was generally our father who came off worst. Granny Bettie knew how to crush him with a few words. So whenever our mother announced she was going to visit her parents, our father claimed he had work to do and shot out of the door.

Granny Bettie and Granddad Alfie still lived on the land where my mother had grown up, but all the things that had made it so special – the old bus, Granddad Alfie's forest and the plantation – had become mere ghosts of their former selves. My mother spoke fondly of the way it used to be when she was a child, but now it had fallen into decline, and so had our granddad, who was bedridden and paralysed from the neck down by multiple sclerosis.

Granny Bettie had let loose her horses and goats in the hope that they could eat through the overgrown grass and weeds that she could no longer clear, but they seemed more interested in eating what was left of the fences.

My mother and Granny Bettie would go out to chase a horse for Frankie to ride on, while I would stay indoors with Granddad Alfie. He would be propped up on his bed and I would perch beside him, holding onto his pipe and listening to his stories. He had taught me how to stuff his pipe with tobacco, light up, and then keep it within an inch of his mouth in between puffs. I'd have a pint of lemon squash at hand, since I choked while trying to keep it alight. Granddad Alfie would teach me his favourite swear words, and how to blow a smoke ring the size of a doughnut. Then he would tell me and Frankie ghost stories, each one of them more terrifying than the last and, according to him, all true.

Granny Bettie would scoff. 'Stop telling them ghost stories, you old fool, filling the children's heads with rubbish. Listen to me you two, when you're dead, you're dead, there's no such a thing as a ghost.'

'God strike me blind, Bettie,' Granddad Alfie cackled. 'When I do drop dead, I'm gonna come back here and kick you right square up the arse!'

'Drop dead then!'

Just after my sixth birthday, he did.

Custom dictated that we had to stay at Granny Bettie's home until the funeral was over. Granddad Alfie was laid out as a centrepiece in the spare room, and in shifts my mother and her family grieved at his side, twenty-four hours a day, until the day of the funeral.

It was a time of sleepless nights, endless pots of coffee and plates of biscuits. During those weeks, friends and family from miles around travelled to pay their last respects, share their stories and say goodbye to Alfie. The old field hadn't seen so many people in years.

I loved listening to them laughing over their memories of him. One told of the bonfire night – which was also his birthday – when Alfie had brought home a swan and cooked it for the guests, much to Granny Bettie's disgust.

My mother was devastated. Her father was the only person who had really understood her and been on her side, and now he was gone. With our father still in prison, she mentally vanished, lying awake each night, never speaking a word and staring blankly into the TV till morning. We would get up to find her lying on the couch, where we had left her when we said goodnight.

Though I loved my father, and wanted to see him, as his release date approached my fear of his violence grew greater every day. When he walked in two months after Granddad Alfie had died he seemed almost a stranger after so long away, and I felt suddenly shy, watching him take my mother in his arms and kiss her, before ruffling my hair and throwing Frankie in the air.

The prison gruel seemed to have agreed with him because he was even more barrel-bodied than before. His sideburns had turned into badger grey horns. He was the image of the 'Pop-up Pirate' Frankie and I played with.

Our mother prepared a slap-up roast to celebrate his return, even managing to root out a couple of old Christmas crackers she had stashed away. They were a ploy to distract us from her 'experimental' cooking; the only thing not scorched as black as a witch's heart were the sprouts, which gave off a festive, yet nuclear green glow. We sat around Mum's American-style Diner table, Frankie and I holding our noses as we forced them down.

That afternoon Frankie and I were outside playing when my father called us both into the house. 'I've got a present for you two, come quick,' he said. We wiped our muddy hands on our clothes and rushed back indoors.

Mother was standing in the kitchen, her back turned and hair messed up on one side of her head. She was quietly cursing to herself, while wrapping her arm in a wet tea towel. Frankie rushed past her and into the lounge. 'What is it? Give it to me,' she yelled.

Something was dreadfully wrong; I could sense it. I needed to see my mother's face, but she kept turning away. I was scared. Reluctantly I followed Frankie, who was sitting on our father's lap, holding a huge, bronze trophy, with two gold-plated boxers welded onto the top.

My father took hold of the ugly thing and raised it above his head. There was a whimper from my mother behind me. 'Leave off, Frank.' He ignored her, rose from his seat, dropped the trophy to Frankie and tapped the back of my head as he passed me on his way to the kitchen.

Confused, I stood, waiting for him to explain.

After some angry murmurs from the kitchen, he returned

with my mother, and pushed her onto the couch. He grabbed hold of Frankie, lifting her into my mother's arms, and then picked me up in a fireman's lift, bringing me over to his chair. He sat, legs astride, pulling me to him so that I was standing between his powerful thighs.

'Now, stand her up like this, Bettie,' he said to my mother.

Mother put Frankie in the same position, between her legs.

Frankie and I looked at each other from across the room.

'Right,' he roared. 'The winner gets the trophy.'

'Why?' asked Frankie.

'Because your father's an evil fucking bastard,' snapped our mother.

My father's grip almost ripped the skin right from my shoulders as I struggled to pull myself from his arms. 'I'm not doing it,' I said.

His voice was low and livid. 'If you don't, I'll give both of you the biggest hiding you've ever had.' Then he changed tack. 'Don't you want to help your brother, Frankie? Do you want to see him get the shit beat out of him every day when he grows up?'

'No!'

'Well then.'

He'd got us, and he knew it.

He pulled the T-shirt from over my head, yanking me to an upright position between his legs.

'Now, the rules. This trophy for a start ain't worthy of somebody who can't throw a good punch. So show no mercy, aim to hurt, and no stopping until you hear the bell. Stop before the bell, you lose, stop fighting, you lose, break the rules, or start crying, you lose.'

We had no choice. It was fight one another or get beaten by our father, and we both knew which was worse. And so we went in fighting; we bit, kicked, punched, clawed and tore at each other as brutally as we could, praying that anytime soon he would sound the bell. But before he did, I lost, sobbing uncontrollably, and breaking every single one of the rules.

Furious at my shameful defeat at the hands of a girl – even though she was twice my size – he beat me as hard as he could, before handing the trophy to Frankie. But she refused to wave it in my face, as he ordered her to do.

He called it a game, and even gave it a name, 'Trophy Sunday'. Every Sunday we were made to fight, and every Sunday Frankie won. She was her father's girl and more worthy of his name than I could ever have been. And every week, after she won, my father would beat the living daylights out of me for losing.

Frankie couldn't stand to hold the trophy; she loathed the sight of the thing. In any case, it was never really either of ours, it was a prize my father had won years earlier, and straight after the weekly battering it would be placed back upon the mantle at his bedside.

Frankie and I held no grudges against each other. We fought because we had no choice, and Frankie would do all she could to save me from him when he chased me through the house after our fight.

After that he beat me more often than he ever had before. He never needed much of an excuse, anything and everything I did seemed to upset him. Even the sight of me disgusted him. I learned to make myself scarce whenever he came home, often hiding out in the tool shed until dark, to avoid the moment he would fetch his old boxing gloves from the bedroom.

Unable to bear what he was doing, and unable to stop him, our mother chose to lock herself away from the daily 'training' sessions and the screams that accompanied it.

But she did manage to give me a few hours of respite each day, by putting us both into a little school down the road.

Had prison changed my father? I don't know what happened to him inside, what things he saw or experienced. He certainly never would have shared this sort of information with me. But what was certain was that the violence that was always latent in him now seemed to hover closer to the surface. It took less to wind him up and it took him longer to cool down. I had always been intimidated by my father, but now I was downright terrified of him. And I had good reason to be.

6

A School and a Big City

I was five and Frankie was six, but my mother managed to wangle us both into Hawkswood Primary School as twins.

On our first morning our mother tucked my shirt in at the back, while simultaneously ripping a brush through Frankie's hair.

'Now, for God's sake, don't go telling them what you are.'

'Why?' squeaked Frankie, holding on to her scalp for dear life.

'Cos they will kick you out on your arses. Now, Mikey, how old are you?'

I stood tall and replied as if she was a drill sergeant.

'I'm six years old and share a birthday with Frankie.'

'That's right, baby.' She leaned towards me, pinched my cheeks and gave me a congratulatory kiss for remembering. Her rare display of physical affection took me by surprise and I blushed with pleasure. 'If anybody asks, that's all you have to tell them, all right?'

Frankie jumped down from the stool and grabbed our lunch boxes.

'All right,' we chorused.

Our mother gave a proud smile, looking us up and down.

'Come on then, you herbs, I don't want to make you late on the first day.'

Like all Gypsy children before us, we had been brought up not to trust Gorgias. And more than anything else, Gypsies don't trust Gorgia schooling. Not just because they believe they don't need a formal education to get by, but because they fear their children will be influenced by the Gorgias, learning too much of their lifestyle and changing them as a people for ever. The Gypsy race is an old-fashioned and, sadly, a very bitter one. They live, breathe, sleep, grieve, love and care for only their own people. They don't like or trust the ways of others and don't have contact or friendships with other races, afraid that one day they will be forced to turn their backs on their once proud way of life and become like any other.

The roots of this go back to the many years of persecution and hatred the Gypsies have suffered, all over the world. They have rarely been liked or tolerated anywhere. Five hundred years ago it was commonplace to see a Gypsy staked upon London Bridge and during every religious war Gypsies were first in the firing line, cast as heathens and godless magicians. In the Second World War many were left as sitting ducks, banging on farmers' doors for sanctuary during Hitler's raids, thrown into prisons and concentration camps to be tortured and killed.

Given this history, Gypsies believe, perhaps understandably, that they have only managed to survive by remaining insular and rejecting the rest of the world. And so, sadly, the prejudices on both sides have only deepened. It is tragic, both for the Gypsies who distrust and hate, and for the other races that never get to see the more human, generous, side of the Romanies.

None of the other Gypsy children in our area went

to school. For the most part, Gypsies were left alone by education officials reluctant to set foot in the local camps. But we lived in a bungalow, where the piles of tarmac, the scrap and my father's bright orange cargo lorry parked on the drive were already aggravating the neighbours. We were bound to be reported, sooner or later.

But my mother wanted us to go. Our father and our grandparents on both sides were unable to read and write. Mum could write a bit, but only using phonetic spelling and in capital letters. She wanted more for us, welcoming the idea of us learning to read and write, while at the same time keeping us out of our father's firing line.

We lasted two weeks.

Within two days, Frankie had brought home the contents of our teacher's stationery drawer and I had stolen a goldfish. I'd reached into the head teacher's, Mrs Trout's, private tank during lunch break, and shoved the little stowaway into my pocket. It died during story time about a half hour or so later and, feeling guilty about being a murderer, I confessed.

A bemused Mrs Trout ordered that from now on, every single lunchtime, she would come and sit between us until we had finished our food, to ensure that we would never be able to repeat such behaviour again. From then on we sat either side of her with our dinner trays, staring wide-eyed as she tucked into her salad bowl with her loose-fitting dentures threatening to pop out of her mouth.

Then came the questions.

'So, how old are you then, Mikey?'

I let out a very small scream. 'I'm six years old and share a birthday with Frankie!'

'Really? That's very interesting.'

'Why?' snapped Frankie.

'Because, my dear, you are so much bigger than your brother is.'

The three of us sat, quietly chewing on our food. I felt a bead of sweat tumble from my forehead.

'I'll need to speak to your mummy after school. Do you think she will be available?'

'Nope,' replied Frankie, sucking on a buttered roll.

'And why not?'

Frankie lifted her head, with a pool of butter spreading across her cheeks.

'Because she thinks you're a cunt.'

Mrs Trout, cheeks scarlet, lifted her tray and moved stiffly to another table. Frankie giggled to herself, making dolphin noises as she slurped her soup.

Later that week a woman who called herself Aunt Gertie appeared in the playground and began paying me and Frankie daily visits. The teachers approached one day and asked us if she was a relative. Although we'd never seen her before, we nodded enthusiastically. We were brought up to call any adults aunt or uncle; it was considered good manners.

Tired of our tendency to stuff anything we could lay our hands on into our pockets, Mrs Trout and her staff were only too happy to have someone there to keep us out of trouble.

We liked Aunt Gertie; she taught us some ripe swear words and never once arrived without some smuggled toys and sweets. So when, one dinner hour, she suggested we go for a walk, we thought it was a great idea.

We were about a mile away when two police cars pulled onto the pavement next to us. Frankie and I were put into one of them while Aunt Gertie was slammed against a wall and arrested for child abduction.

With all the faceless relatives we already had, it was hard for us to keep track of who was or was not part of our family. But Aunt Gertie, we discovered, was definitely not. She was, in fact, just a local nutter who had taken a liking to us.

After that brief foray into school, we found ourselves back at home again, forbidden to leave the house, while Mother dealt with the trauma the school had put her and her kids through. Frankie and I didn't really mind, we were just happy not to have to wake up so early. We went back to amusing ourselves at home once more.

Thrown on our own resources, with only one another to play with, Frankie and I turned to our toys for company. They became our best friends, taking on personalities of their own. For Frankie it was Jesus, the Barbies and the brand-new Cabbage Patch dolls she continued to receive courtesy of Old Noah. For me, apart from my Action Man tank, which I was using as a urinal, there was a glow in the dark Dracula doll, a crocodile oven mitt I named Grandma Buggins, and, of course, my He-Man figures. My favourite toy of all was He-Man's arch nemesis, Skeletor, the muscle-bound, blue-skinned villain with a skeleton's face and a goat's head on a stick as his choice weapon. I loved him so much, that the only reason I wanted the others was so that he could beat them up or bury them alive in the garden. I never left the house or went on a trip without smuggling him in with me somewhere.

Most days Barbie and her friends invited He-Man and his pals to dinner. I'd even raid Frankie's dolls' clothes box to dress them formally for the occasion. The problem was they had such muscle-bound torsos that nothing fitted, so I improvised by cutting three holes in the end of each of my socks to make evening gowns for them.

But our favourite game together was still the forbidden Aunt Sadly. I would wear one of Frankie's nightdresses and her now disused navy school tights, with small stones shoved down the legs to look like varicose veins, just like Mrs Trout's. Then, after Frankie had taught me how to behave like a lady, I would stay in the shop, while my 'niece' went off on a shopping spree around the house.

Early one morning we were at this game while our parents were still asleep. Frankie was putting on my make-up in the bathroom, when we heard stirring from the main bedroom. Our father was awake and was making his way through the house to the bathroom. I fell backwards into Frankie, wriggling my shoulder blades and pointing towards the knot where the nightdress was tied on at the back of my neck. 'Untie it, quick,' I whispered.

Frankie's fingers fumbled and tugged, pulling it tighter in her panic, and half-strangling me. I rammed my face into a dry bath towel and scraped frantically at my make-up.

'What the fuck, are you doing in there?'

Frankie pushed out a grunting sound, 'Can you wait a minute, Dad, I'm on the toilet.'

'I know you're both in there. Open the door – now.'

Reluctantly Frankie unlocked the door.

He barged in to find us both in glamorous dress and full make-up, only mine was now smeared all over my face.

Our father's violent outbursts were becoming more frequent and more vicious, not just when he was training me, but whenever the monster within took him over. And this was one of those times.

I was pulled into the beating room, the new and well-deserved name for my bedroom. And after the thrashing I got that day we had to kill off Aunt Sadly; her presence around the house was far too risky. We gave her a funeral, and laid her to rest out in the garden along with the rest of the bodies. We both missed her.

I envied my sister. She was untouchable because she was a girl. I adored her, worshipped her and hated her all at the same time. She was never at the end of a punch, a belt, or a boot, never hated, humiliated or jeered at. She was my father's daughter, more like him than I could ever be, and safe, because of her sex.

Old Granddad Noah was looming over my father like a spectre, reminding him constantly of his lack of worth compared to Tory and now Tory's strapping sons. And I just rubbed salt in the wound. Day by day my father's revulsion for me grew and my body became a mass of bruises, new layered on top of the old.

Still, in some respects the training worked. In time I learned to withstand most of his punches without crying out or flinching. But rather than being pleased with me, he saw this as a fresh challenge. If I didn't scream with pain, he wouldn't be satisfied. He searched for ways to 'test' me, with belts, sticks, boot-heels and even Barbie dolls, whipped across my legs, leaving marks that made the blood rise from my skin. In truth, my father wasn't testing me, or training me, he was punishing me for failing him. I wasn't the son he dreamed of, and he was never going to forgive me for that.

By the time I was six years old I wasn't even allowed to be seen in his presence or mutter a word, unless he addressed me first. I was a silent ghost of a child, terrified of provoking his rage, just by existing.

When I was six and a half, our mother fell ill and was taken to hospital. Granny Bettie was sent to look after us until she came home, reassuring us that she would be fine and that she was bringing back a surprise, and a week or so later, she did; a new baby brother for us. We had no idea where babies came from, and it was not for us to ask, unless we wanted a clip around the ear. We could only assume that they had bought baby Henry-Joe from the hospital, the same way Frankie would buy one from (the late) Aunt Sadly's shop.

Even as a newborn, it was apparent that Henry-Joe shared our mother's looks. He was white-skinned and red-haired with a head the shape of a perfect little apple. Nothing like my father's breed at all.

'He's one of us, Frank, you can't deny it', croaked my granny Bettie on his arrival.

And he couldn't. My mother's grief for her own father was transformed into love for a child she was determined my father and his awful family would stay away from. And Henry-Joe's appearance, attributes and constant surveillance from my mother's side saved him. My father accepted he was still without an heir.

As for Frankie and I, we regarded the new arrival with a mixture of awe, affection and horror. We had never heard a baby cry so much. He didn't stop, especially at night, when one of our parents would have to get into the car and drive him around, just to get him back off to sleep.

I found Henry-Joe fascinating and was unable to take my eyes off him when our mother held him on her lap. Frankie, feeling a little jealous, chose to resurrect old Jesus from under her bed. His ageing vibrations and squawks sounded more and more like a cement mixer, but he caused Frankie a lot less grief than Henry-Joe did our parents. Frankie and I would stuff our ears with socks before we went to sleep, just to avoid his midnight screams.

Late one night, a few weeks after Henry-Joe's birth, our father's bellow vibrated down the hallway. 'Come on, wake up! We're going to London to see the lights.' We rarely ever left our house, but every now and then our father did things like this – taking us all off at midnight, on a whim.

I jumped out of bed and scuttled into the lounge. My mother was wrestling with a wailing Henry-Joe and a nappy, while applying a slick of eyeliner at the same time.

'Quickly, grab your clothes and put on something warm.'

I ran into Frankie's room; she was pulling a pair of her leggings onto Jesus. 'I'm gonna take him to see Big Ben,' she said, and in a squeaky baby voice to Jesus, 'Yes I is, baby, I'm taking you to see the Queen.'

I tore back to my room, nearly running head-on into the doorframe with excitement. I reached into my drawer and put on my favourite Darth Vader costume pyjamas and grabbed Skeletor from his house.

'Hurry up then,' shouted our mother, as Henry-Joe wriggled and wailed in her arms. We bounded down the hall, clutching our treasured possessions. 'And bring a quilt each to keep you warm.'

I ran back, grabbing my quilt and wrapping it around my shoulders like a mammoth ermine. Through the window I could hear my father revving the engine of the car.

The night was cold and crisp as Frankie and I jumped into the car, grinning at each other from across the back seats, shaking and kicking our legs with delight. A couple of miles from home Henry-Joe's cries became whimpers and he went off to sleep. Frankie and I sat barefoot in the back, miming with our toys to my mother's Barbra Streisand tape.

With Frankie as puppeteer, Jesus could do a mean Barbra impersonation, although I'm sure if he was alive he would have been utterly humiliated by the whole experience.

I loved being in the car at night; the quiet hum beneath my bare feet, and the strobes of the motorway lamps and catseyes reflecting from my window sent me into a deep, sombre trance.

Skeletor sat in my lap, contemplating his next overturn of the world as I rested my head against the window to feel its cold vibration. The sound of soothing saxophones buzzed from our mother's UB40 tape mix. My father lit up his umpteenth cigarette, his gold rings clicking against the glass as he flicked away the excess ash. I pulled the duvet up around my face, holding in the warmth close to my chin.

London: the home of Mary Poppins, Oliver Twist and that witch out of *Bedknobs and Broomsticks*. I knew all the songs from the films, but wondered if it could really be the same as in the movies.

I drifted in and out of sleep, until I was given a heavy nudge by my sister. 'Wake up quick. Look at them.'

She leaned over my lap, pointing at a huge column guarded by four great black lions. They managed to appear majestic, heroic and sinister all at once. Our faces pressed against the rear window as we left them behind. An old man sat between one of the monster's front paws, like a cub in his protection, resting his weary head on its stone chest. It reminded me of me, held between my father's legs.

A gut-wrenching sadness came over me. I looked over at my father, who was pulling a cigarette from his lips and spinning some story about how years ago, a witch had put the lions there and turned them to stone. 'But late at night, they come back to life to hunt for little boys and girls,' he finished, with a sinister laugh.

I looked back to check. It was late now, and yet the beasts were still frozen in a black death. I said nothing, knowing that, where my father was concerned, I could never be right.

I had caught him from time to time, watching me as I played, talked to Skeletor and dozed. His eyes were deep-set and black, with whites as yellow as poison. Like a Gorgon, the monster inside him would glare, freezing me to the spot and turning me to stone.

I sat with my nose against the window. The city outside was so enormous. If I ran from the car now I thought, they could never find me again. I would be free. I could join a gang like Fagin's and spend my days picking pockets. I could come and sit with that lion too, as often as I wanted to. For a moment the prospect seemed so wonderful. But

I knew there was no way to escape. The only place I would be going was back to the bungalow and to my beating room.

One day, I told myself, this great city is where I am going to be. This is where I'll come to.

7

Welcome to Warren Woods

We had been in the bungalow for just over a year when our father arrived home one day with the news that a new Gypsy camp was being built a few miles from where his family were living. He had bought a plot, a brand-new trailer and a new lorry to ship us all there. We were going back to our roots.

And so we packed up and moved to start a new life just a few miles from Tory Manor, in West Sussex.

The road leading up to our new home was long and straight, with trees so high at each side that they met over the roofs of passing cars, creating the impression, to a small boy, of a dark and monstrous forest, split by the road hewn out of its overgrown wilderness.

Frankie was glued to the window on the left and me to the right. I wondered if anyone had ever dared go into the forest to see who lived in there.

'I don't want you two going wandering in these woods,' Mother said, picking a clot of heavy blue mascara from her eye in the rear-view mirror as she manoeuvred Henry-Joe around on her lap. 'Do you hear me?'

'Why?' asked Frankie.

'Because a witch lives there,' snapped our mother.

'I thought so.'

Every now and then we would pass a house buried deep

in the woods as if it had been swallowed up and was being slowly digested by the foliage.

'Will we know anyone who lives here?' asked Frankie, scratching at her frilly dress.

'Yes,' our father said. 'And while your granny Ivy ain't well we have to live here and put you two in school.

'What's wrong with her, Dad?' I asked.

'She just ain't well, Mikey.'

Granny Ivy was always ill. I thought it must have been something to do with her being a midget. I was already taller than she was and she was always using a scary-looking gas mask to help her breathe.

'School?' shouted Frankie. 'But that's for Gorgia children.'

'You two got to go to the school. People will come and take you away if you don't,' our mother said, looking up from her vanity case, Henry-Joe now tucked under her arm. 'Anyway, you'll be there with the other children from the site. You won't be the only ones. And I'm putting you in as twins again, so you'll be together.'

We knew we were nearly there, because mother had applied a thick layer of coral lipstick and was putting on yet more of her blue mascara.

'When do we start?' Frankie asked.

'Monday morning. Me and your aunt Nancy are gonna take turns taking you all there and back.'

'Are Olive and Twizzel moving here too?'

'For fuck's sake, yes!' bellowed our father. 'Now get your fucking coats on.'

Frankie gave an exited wince, wriggling and kicking her feet. We hadn't seen our cousins since Frankie loaded their knickers with lime jelly while they slept when they'd visited us at the bungalow.

The indicator was clicking on my side, but it wasn't for a while that we saw the entrance to our new home. Frankie climbed over my lap for a better look.

They had somehow managed to bulldoze deep into the wood and make a huge open space. It was bigger than anything I had ever seen before. So huge I could not see how far back it went. It looked as if a giant meteor had fallen from the sky and crashed here, clearing the space. After the darkness of the forest, the light above the clearing shone through so brightly that our eyes had to adjust.

Our car was greeted by the owner, a man with a face like a sack of potatoes, who leaned through the window to greet us. As he spoke to our parents, Frankie and I stared in wonder. The clearing was like a huge swamp. Not a blade of grass, not a tree in sight, but endless mud and water and several towering pillars, with iron steps at the sides and thick electric cables balancing from the top. I wondered if it was one this size that had hurt our mother.

We got out of the car and I stood against the wall, which was at least three times my size. On it hung a huge white sign with big red letters stuck onto it with melted rubber: Welcome Travellers to Warren Woods Caravan Park.

While our father parked the lorry, our mother lifted Henry-Joe close to her chest and ushered us towards the empty space we were to call home. Our father staggered back towards us through a sea of mud.

'This is it, you herbs,' said our mother. I liked it when she called us her herbs, because it meant she was in a good mood. We stared at our piece of land. There was a thread of red string all around the outside of it, to mark where our walls would be. The ground within it had been levelled off. It was as big as a field, and with one of the electric totem poles sticking out of it, it looked as if a great pirate ship had just sunk in the middle.

Frankie pulled herself free from Mother's grasp, screaming for joy, and managed three steps before falling face down in a foot of mud. There was a cartoon farting noise and I fell about laughing, almost wetting myself.

Due to its size, our new trailer was delivered to us in two halves, but was still only a fraction of the space we'd had in the bungalow. Frankie and I were back to sharing a bedroom, so narrow our father could barely fit through the door. We had bunk beds once again, and being the most accident-prone, I was banished to the bottom.

Despite being brand new, the trailer was very like the last one inside; all brown with a splat of orange and fake wood walls. And once they had put it together and laid the carpet, Frankie and I were stuck inside for several days, like a couple of prisoners. It rained non-stop, so there was no way our mother was going to let us go outside and then tread mud all over her new bright pink carpet.

We had an electric box, connected to a cable that ran straight from the pole, so we were able to keep warm and watch videos. Which we did, all day. We wouldn't hear from our parents until they came in after dark with either a bucket of Kentucky Fried Chicken, or fish and chips. We peered out of the window from the couch and watched the lorries dumping piles of rocks all over the place while my father and the other men spread them across the mud. Hovering a few feet from our father was our mother, with

Henry-Joe strapped onto her front and carrying a large funeral umbrella to ward off the rain.

Other trailers arrived and disappeared into the furthest reaches of the crater, and other men appeared to help with the stone-shifting. Slowly the camp was taking shape.

Meanwhile I had two things to dread. School, on Monday, and – far worse – my first night at the boxing club, down the road from Uncle Tory's house, three days later. Every time my father came into the trailer he reminded me about it.

One afternoon he burst in and flicked the switch to the kettle.

I was in mid-wail, wearing a pillowslip as a bonnet, being an orphan baby that Olive, Twizzel and Frankie had found in the woods. He stood over me; his glare tearing me apart, making me feel worthless and humiliated. I'd have preferred it if he'd beaten me to a pulp.

'Ready to fight?'

The mention of it made my insides collapse. 'Yep,' I replied, trying to sound enthusiastic and failing miserably.

I pulled the bonnet from my head, and ran from the room. Knowing he was likely to land a good kick on me, I ran past him with one hand on each buttock cheek, furious with myself for being caught out once again.

I wished I could be more like Uncle Tory's sons, Tory and Noah. Tough, fighting boys who made their dad proud. I was nothing like them – and my father knew it. I was a hopeless boxer and he knew that too. Frankie still won the trophy every Sunday. I thought maybe he should take her.

Two days later we started at St Luke's Primary School, a couple of miles up the road, along with a handful of

other children from our camp. The local education officers here were, apparently, more scrupulous than those in
our last home had been, and would regularly turn up in
the local Gypsy camps, demanding that the children be
sent to school.

St Luke's had known we would be coming, and the
Gorgia parents there had demanded that we be kept
separate from their children. A compromise had been
agreed: we were taught separately during the morning, and
joined the regular classes in the afternoons.

For the morning shift, we were put into our own special
classroom, which was so small that it may well have
formerly been the broom closet, and supplied with our own
special teacher: Mrs McAndrew, a vision in autumnal
shades, with arms like sacks of oranges and hair like a
bird's nest.

As well as Frankie and me, there were Olive and Twizzel,
Jamie-Leigh Bowers and three of the five Donoghue children.

The Donoghues were Irish Travellers who had recently
moved to the far end of our camp and claimed to be the
new breed of Gypsy. We were a dark-skinned race, apart
from our mother. They had skin like lard, strawberry-blond
hair and were smothered in freckles.

Most non-travellers put all travelling people in the same
category. But the Romanies and the Irish Travellers are
worlds apart. Both races have very proud origins. But the
Romanies were around for centuries before the Irish
Travellers existed. For many years the Irish Travellers were
workers for the Romany people. Then, as time passed, they
went their own way, while mimicking the values and way
of life of the Romanies. Since then the Irish Travellers have

prospered, while nursing a deep dislike of the Romany people who were once their masters. Today the Romanies are wary wherever they go, in case there are Irish Travellers around to attack them. The two races have nothing but contempt for one another, and the war between them has gone a long way towards destroying the Gypsy culture.

When they first met, Tyrone Donoghue shook my father's hand and said, 'We Irish are gonna take over this country, Frank.'

People didn't take him seriously, because he looked so ridiculous. He was a little ferret-faced man, strutting about. But despite the general hostility between our two peoples, my father took to him right away and they often went to the pub together in the evenings.

The Donoghue children spoke with such a thick Irish accent that we couldn't understand them, even after two weeks. And the teacher had the same problem. She spoke to all of us as if we were retarded.

'The cat (long pause) sat (even longer pause) on the mat. See, children?'

'Oh, for fuck's sake.' Jamie-Leigh was never short of words.

'Language, Miss Bowers!' But Mrs McAndrew's soft voice was no match for Jamie-Leigh.

She was the single prettiest girl I had ever seen. She looked like a Gypsy princess. Her pitch-black hair fell about her waist like an oil spill and her eyes were such a pure green that she looked like an angel. Then she would open her mouth and out would come the vocabulary of a fifty-year-old hooker.

Even in the mixed classes where we spent the afternoons

she wouldn't think twice about hollering out questions, using the c-word in every sentence, and farting violently. She was vile, but I thought she was amazing. I envied her so much it made me gag. Here was me, near mute, chin tucked into the neck of my jumper, hair brushed forward over my eyes, trying my very best to disappear, while she walked tall and didn't give a damn what people thought of her. She knew she was great, and these people were not going to convince her otherwise.

Jamie-Leigh, Frankie and I were all in the same class. Frankie and I had got in as twins again, despite the difference in our size. And Jamie-Leigh, who was younger than me, had somehow been wangled in by her mother, Audrey, so that she could be near us.

On our first day Mrs Kerr, the afternoon teacher, announced the term's topic.

She was Scottish and her Rs rolled and curled from her tongue. 'The topic for all of us this term is Ancient Egypt.'

'What, like the pyramids and that?' said Frankie.

'Yes. And that and a whole lot more, Miss Walsh. Pharaohs, mummies, curses, the Nile – all of it. And you are going to pick your favourite part to research.'

Jamie-Leigh leaned towards my ear. 'She sounds like that cunt Lorraine Kelly.'

That was the final straw for Mrs Kerr.

'Miss Bowers, you will do your work in the afternoons at my desk. I rarely use it, and I know you'll love the peace and quiet, as will I. Grab your stuff, pet.'

A tut and a kiss of the teeth as Jamie-Leigh dragged herself over. As soon as she sat down at the teacher's desk, she saw the benefits of her new, high-status seat; it was ideal for grabbing the attention of the entire class. Mrs Kerr was clearly going to live to regret moving her most disruptive pupil.

While Jamie-Leigh loved the limelight, the burglary side of primary education was more Frankie's thing. Tugging Jamie-Leigh along with her, she would wait for break time to go through everyone's drawers searching for the goodies every kid was after: iron-on Batman stickers.

While Frankie and Jamie-Leigh were hard at work, Mrs Kerr would make her way outdoors and stand at the playground gates for a cigarette, before putting on her roller-skates and racing around the tarmac with the older children. She must have been over forty. I couldn't imagine my Mother ever doing anything like that, and she was only twenty-six.

The majority of our time at school was spent either fighting with the Gorgia children, or teaching Mrs McAndrew our language. She was far more interested in learning from us than in teaching us anything. Romany, an ancient language, is still used by Gypsies, but only in combination with English. Romany makes up about 60 per cent of Gypsy dialect, because many words have been forgotten over time. So a Gypsy's English vocabulary is often at the same level as a five-year-old child's.

A few Romany words are recognised outside the Gypsy community. For instance, the word *chavi* means a young boy but has been adapted by the outside world into chav, used to describe a rough, working-class or tasteless person. And cushti, which means good, or a good feeling, was used by Del Boy in *Only Fools and Horses*. But most of our language is unknown to outsiders. Mrs McAndrew seemed fascinated and asked us to teach her some of our words. She even wrote a Gypsy song.

> Dordie, dordie, dik-ka-kye,
> Blackbird sing and poofter cry,
> Dordie, dordie, dik-ka-kye,
> Kecker, rocker, nixies.

The translation to this piece, shows just how little sense it makes:

> Surprised, surprised, look over there,
> Blackbird sing and poofter cry,
> Surprised, surprised, look over there,
> Don't say a thing.

That is, 'O my gosh, look over there, there's a blackbird and a poof crying. Don't tell anyone.'

It seemed we were just as bad at playing teacher as she was. Why she added the word poofter I have no idea. It's not a Romany word, though perhaps she thought it was.

8

The Club

My father opened the passenger door of the car, hurling a huge leather bag in after me.

Stuffed inside were a pair of second-hand boxing gloves that reeked of sweat and a sickly yellow, neatly pressed pair of cousin Tory's old shorts.

Frankie pushed her chubby face up against the window as my father lit up a cigarette and started the engine. He leaned over his shoulder, pushing smoke through his nostrils as he started to reverse off the plot.

'See you later,' she mouthed. I swallowed hard and closed my eyes. I was dreading this drive almost as much as what was waiting for me at the other end.

'Your granddad Noah's gonna be there. Your uncle Tory, young Tory and Noah, Nelson Collins, Uncle Joseph . . .'

My father was in full flow, but with each new name my spirits sank lower. I stared hard at him as he spoke, nodding furiously and trying my best to look interested. But I was terrified. As we slowed down and turned into the entrance of the boxing club my stomach heaved.

My father's entourage clustered around him as soon as he stepped from the car. I slid the bag from the passenger seat and heaved it onto my shoulder. It was so big I'd have tripped over it any other way, but this way it covered my face, too.

I trundled along next to him, like a bag boy with a local celebrity. Everyone we ran into stopped to talk to him.

Inside we ran into Tyrone Donoghue. 'You following your father's footsteps then, boy?' he grinned. He turned to my father. 'I've had my Paddy in here for a year now.'

Tyrone had two sons and, bizarrely, he had named them both Paddy. The older Paddy was thirteen and at secondary school age, although he had never been to one and couldn't even write his name. I watched him carry his sports bag into the club. He looked a lot more dignified than I did. His kit was already on, his bag appeared as light as a pillowcase and his hair was brushed upward into thick yellow spikes.

Someone dug his hand into my free shoulder. 'Going to grow up a fighting man like your dad then?' I turned around to see a man with a face like a rolled-up pair of socks, with an ear missing and an eye like a boiled onion. I tried not to stare.

'You're nothing but a cunt you is! Don't you remember your Uncle Levoy?' he laughed.

I knew so many Levoys at this point in my life they all seemed to blend into one, but this monster of a man I could have never forgotten. He was notorious for the brutal ways he found of torturing his enemies.

Uncle Tory met us at the main doors of the club. From inside I could hear thuds, punches and the snap of skipping ropes. The stench of what I know now was testosterone and sweat was so thick it stuck to my face like cling film.

An eruption of panic was building up inside me and I started to tremble. The base of my throat started to fill with sick and I was afraid I would faint.

'Right then, you ready?' My father looked down at me expectantly.

'Yep.'

'Come on then, let's get you changed.'

The disgusting smell of the club grew thicker as we stepped in, and the sounds of hisses and grunts bounced off the walls. I dragged my feet as we marched through the main hallway, which was so dark it was like an old ghost train, with sickly yellow walls and a carpet that was sticky and matted.

As the changing-room door creaked open, I saw that Granddad Noah and Uncle Joseph were sitting inside on a bench, smoking cigars and holding cans of bitter, as if they were in the local pub.

My father joined them as I stripped off reluctantly, wishing I could be anywhere but where I was. I turned to face them. The yellow shorts, with TORY WALSH stitched in gold letters across the front, came to just under my armpits.

Joseph, a carbon copy of Granddad Noah, with the same electric blue eyes, grinned. 'You look the part, Mikey. Don't he look the part, Dad?'

Old Noah turned to me. 'He looks just like his dad did at his age, proper little fighting man. When you win this I'll get you some shorts with your name on the front.'

My father smiled at me and got down onto the floor to help me lace my boots. He was so anxious to impress his father. I could tell from the way he agreed with everything the old man said.

'See you in the ring, Mikey,' said Old Noah. Joseph smiled and mouthed 'good luck' as he left the room.

'See,' said my father. 'They're all here to watch you beat this feller tonight.'

'What's he like, Dad?'

'A fool, just a little Irish cunt. One hit, my boy, and he'll go down like a sack of potatoes, I promise you.'

That's when I realised they had chosen Paddy Donoghue for me to fight. A boy more than twice my age, and size.

'But he's older than me, Dad.'

My father tightened his grip on my forearm, which made the blood rush to my fingertips. He swung me towards him. I was so close I could see the burnt patches in his leathery skin, from his years of shovelling tarmac. His look was icy. 'Makes no difference if he's older than you, you're going in that ring and beating that boy. Don't you let me down or I'll beat you all the way to Basingstoke.'

'I won't, Dad.'

'Take an oath you won't.'

'On my life I won't.' I tried not to whine, as I promised him the impossible.

There was a long pause. My father's breath hung like a sleeping dragon's in the putrid air and I could feel the heat from his body. He tucked in the laces of my gloves, then stood up and left the room, without looking at me again.

This conversation was over. I was to get in the ring with Paddy Donoghue, and I *had* to win.

The match lasted around fifteen seconds.

Each second had counted another punch thrown by Paddy, and every one landed with a leather-clad thud on my head.

I had been put into the ring with a much more experienced, older boy, who was at least a foot taller than me, and more than happy to beat the crap out of a young Walsh boy. By the time Uncle Tory bellowed 'stop' I had completely lost control. My ill-fitting gloves had been thrown off and I was wailing and clinging on to Paddy to stop him from throwing yet another humiliating punch at my head.

We were prised apart. My body hurt, my head was throbbing and there was blood splashed across my face. I tried – and I failed – to hold back my tears as I made my way through the ropes and past the crowd and my father, who wouldn't even look at me.

I made my way back to the changing room, which was empty. I couldn't stop crying and I started yelling at myself. 'Shut up! Please shut up!' I felt as if I were about to faint. I sat down and took a deep breath, then took my clothes out of the bag and slowly started to get dressed. Footsteps grew closer and I could hear my father outside saying his goodbyes, his voice quiet, no doubt shamed by my performance.

I didn't want to leave the changing room, but, after fifteen minutes of dawdling, my hope that my father would come in and reassure me faded.

It was Joseph who came in to find me sitting on the bench. He walked over and sat by my side. He put his giant arm around me and squeezed. 'Are you all right?'

As soon as he said those words I burst into a fit of uncontrollable tears.

'Don't worry, Mikey,' he said, rubbing my back. 'Don't cry my boy. It's going to be all right.'

But I knew it wasn't.

My father opened the door and threw the car keys at me. I slipped out through the crowds, crept across the car park and got into the car to wait for him. I watched as he said his goodbyes and lit a cigarette, before climbing into the driver's seat.

I spent the first part of the journey home staring out of the window. I was so petrified my chest was pounding and my breathing was getting louder. Despite the voice in my head screaming at me to stay quiet, a huge whimper escaped.

'What's the matter with you?' my father snarled. I shook my head to say that it was nothing.

He drew back his enormous fist and punched me in the ear, as we swerved across the road.

'I can't (PUNCH!) believe (PUNCH) you showed (PUNCH) me up like that.'

'Please don't, Dad, I really tried, please don't.'

'Don't what?' (PUNCH)

He paused and watched as blood began to slide from my nose and into my mouth. My lip started to quiver uncontrollably.

'Are you going to cry? Are you, my boy?' He slapped me hard across the face. 'Go on then.' He slapped me again. The blood from my nose smeared into my eye and splattered across the window.

I couldn't stop the tears, but I made no sound. My father turned to face the road ahead. 'Little poofy boy, that's all you are, my son,' he said. 'Who'd have thought I'd end up with one like you.'

As we pulled into our plot, I opened the car door and

ran for the trailer. I wanted to reach my mother before my father got there.

She was lying on the floor, watching *Dynasty*, with Frankie brushing her hair.

They both gasped when they saw me.

'What the fuck happened to you?' my mother screeched.

My father came in and pushed me out of the way. 'Your son has just been beaten by a boy half his size in front of everybody.'

Had he just forgotten that he was the one who had done this to me? He was lying to her!

And she was taking it all in.

She turned to me. 'Go to bed, Mikey. Get out of my sight.'

Frankie and I climbed into bed and pulled the curtain across the doorway. Not that it disguised any of what was being said. I could hear words like shameful, disgrace, poof and useless being repeated again and again.

'What happened?' whispered Frankie.

I told Frankie about the fight with Paddy. In an instant, her eyes narrowed and in a voice like a foghorn she bellowed, 'Paddy Donoghue is too big to be fighting Mikey, Mum!'

Our father marched to the doorway and ripped back the curtain.

We screamed and pulled the blankets over our heads.

He grabbed me by the leg and ripped me out of the bed. I crashed to the floor and Frankie fell from the top bunk, trying to reach out and grab me by the arm. The carpet burned my back as he pulled me by the feet into the lounge. I kicked and screamed as Frankie held on to my arms, digging her heels into the ground to try to wrench me away from his grasp. Henry-Joe began to cry and mother walked toward the bedroom. I reached out and tried to grab her leg, but couldn't.

My father pointed towards the bedroom. 'Frankie, get one of the nappies from the bag.'

Not daring to disobey, she went to Henry-Joe's baby bag, took out one of his nappies and handed it over.

'Stand up.'

I couldn't. My body had started to convulse, I had lost all control of it.

'Please let him go,' screamed Frankie.

'Take his pants off.'

I kicked my legs and shouted and cried. Frankie hesitated, then took hold of my pants and slid them down my legs, as he lifted me onto his knee. I could barely breathe, my throat was so sore from crying. He pulled the nappy up my legs, then, lifting me by my arms, he threw me across the floor.

'You act like a baby, then I'll treat you like one. Get to bed. I don't want to look at your fucking ugly face again.'

Still weeping, I waddled into the bedroom, climbed into bed and covered myself completely with the covers. At least under there I could be alone.

My parents started to argue and Henry-Joe began to cry again.

'He's only six years old, Frank, what were you thinking of, making him fight that Donoghue boy?'

'I was five when I got in the ring. Your son is a fucking embarrassment.'

'*You're* a fucking embarrassment,' she screamed.

There was a loud thud and she fell to the floor. Frankie came in and shut the door behind her. 'Bastard,' she said quietly, climbing the ladder. 'Fucking old bastard.'

I awoke the next morning in a puddle. I'd been desperate to go to the bathroom, but I didn't dare pass my father to go out to the toilet tent. I waited for him to fall asleep, but he sat in front of the TV late into the night, watching *The Texas Chainsaw Massacre* and, exhausted and aching, I had eventually fallen asleep.

Now I was trapped in my room, desperate to hide my accident. But my father was halfway through a mound of bacon sandwiches and my mother had begun to lose her patience. 'Mikey, if I've got to shout for you one more time . . .'

A moment later my father swooped into the bedroom, yellow-eyed, a bacon sandwich in his fist. 'You've got three seconds to get your arse out of that bed. One, two . . .'

I leaped up, and the Paddy pad slipped down my leg. My father paused, shoved in the last bite of his sandwich, then grabbed my arm and began to drag me outside.

I cried and wailed as he ordered me to strip. I looked around to see a small crowd of familiar faces, stopping in their tracks to see what was going on. My father had grabbed the pressure hose that was used to wash the trucks. He pointed it at me.

The pressure of the jet against my skin was like being trampled on by a pack of horses. The ice-cold water punched me in the ears and face. Then he directed it at my stomach. I threw up, keeling over onto all fours.

When he finally turned it off I crawled back into the

trailer. My teeth were chattering violently and I had to stop to be sick again after swallowing so much of the water.

I crawled back into the bedroom and got myself ready for school.

9

Boot Camp

As I arrived at school that morning, Mrs Kerr said I looked unwell and asked if anything was wrong. My ears were blocked and I could still hear the sound of the water jet. My head and body ached, and I felt sick.

'No,' I told her.

'You stay in here with me this morning, pet,' she said gently.

Frankie and Jamie-Leigh left for Mrs McAndrew's room.

'I know you love to draw,' Mrs Kerr said, 'and I could do with a young man of your talents today. I need you to design me a poster for the class. How does that grab you?'

I made my way over to the desk she was pointing at, where she had put some sheets of paper and a pack of coloured pens. I tried not to knock the back of anyone's chair, or catch anyone's eye. I hated being looked at and I could feel the other children staring at me as if they all knew just how disgusting I was.

I sat, trying to draw, but unable to concentrate. I needed the toilet, but I was terrified to pass the other children again, or draw Mrs Kerr's attention. Paralysed, I wet myself and started to cry.

Mrs Kerr took me to the boys' toilet herself and said that she would be right back with some clean underwear from lost property. When she returned she knelt in front of me to unlace my shoes, then pulled each trainer from my feet. My fingers were too limp to undo my fly. As she went to take my trousers off, I tried to stop her.

'Now, Mikey,' said Mrs Kerr, 'there's no shame in having an accident, we've all had them.'

She undid the zip and tugged at my trousers, revealing the red-frilled knickers – a pair of my mother's – which my father had forced me to wear.

'Mikey, my pet, why are you wearing those?'

'My dad made me wear them.'

'Why?'

'Because I wet the bed last night.'

She spotted the bruises on my legs, and lifted my jumper to follow the trail. Her expression was grim. 'Step into these trousers, pet,' she said.

When I was changed she held my hand and led me out of the toilets and round towards the school office.

'Mikey, I'm so sorry,' she said, 'but I've already phoned your parents to come and collect you. I thought you were unwell and needed to go home.'

My mother came for me. She didn't look at me once, as she led me towards the car. Mrs Kerr followed, trying to explain that the accident had been her fault, as she hadn't noticed I needed to be excused. My mother ignored her.

She said nothing all the way home, and neither did I. I was sitting in the trailer, eating a bowl of cereal, when my father arrived home from work.

'What's he doing home so early?'

I prayed my mother would say nothing.

'He pissed himself again.'

Before I could pull the spoon from my lips my father took two steps forward, raised his arm and punched me hard and square in the mouth, sending both me and the chair hurtling across the floor.

After that I began wetting the bed every night. And every morning, depending on my father's mood, I was publicly stripped and hosed down, or a given a good beating inside the tool shed. His weapons of choice ranged from a belt to a bamboo stick or the heel of his boot. But his bare fists were by far the most painful of all. Sometimes, if he had the time, I was put through both ordeals, being dragged off to the shed and beaten while naked and soaking wet. If it was the weekend his anger would continue throughout the day. He would hit me with whatever happened to be in his hand at the time, a shovel, a broom, or even scalding shovels of tarmac if he'd taken me to work with him.

One Monday he ordered that I stay home from school. 'You're spending too much time with women,' he growled. 'Pampered, that's what you've been, my boy. Too much time around your mother and her lot. There's only one way to get you straightened out. Your granddad's said to leave you with him and Tory for a while.'

We climbed into the truck. 'Every time I see you you're playing with them girls, or with those fucking men of yours,' he said. 'It's time you stopped.'

He meant my modest, but proud collection of He-Man action figures that my mother had bought. From today, he said, they would all be given away. I had to start becoming a man.

A month earlier he had hurled one of them out of the lorry window after noticing it had boobs. 'It's a boy's one,

Dad,' I had shrieked. 'It's Evil Lyn!' I had pestered my mother to get me Skeletor's evil wife for a very long time.

'All right, Mikey,' she had said. 'But let your dad see her and she's pissed on her chips.'

She was right. The moment he set eyes on Evil Lyn she was doomed. After he had lobbed her through the window I stared after her, heartbroken.

Now I was staring out of the window again as he ranted at me, ripping me apart and saying cruel things about my mother. I hoped he would soon run out of steam, or at least pause for breath.

It was an autumn day. I watched the blurred browns and reds as we roared along. I imagined being Evil Lyn, taking flight after being thrown out of the window. My cloak curling, snapping and whipping through the countryside, as I screamed in wicked delight at my freedom.

I laughed out loud.

'What are you doing?'

'Nothing.' Caught out once again I slid back into my seat.

Even though his eyes were on the road for the rest of the journey it felt as if they were boring right through me.

He hated me.

My granddad Noah ran the scrapyard, with Tory and Joseph. Tory's sons, young Tory and Noah, worked there too, men before they were thirteen, with thoughts of school long abandoned.

I always wondered why my father hadn't joined his father and brothers, who all lived and worked together. Later I came to understand that his family didn't trust him in the business and he didn't want to be there – he was intent on going it alone and proving himself to his father.

We pulled into the yard just behind Uncle Joseph. My father turned off the motor and jumped out. 'How yer doing boyeee?' he called to Uncle Joseph. Then he turned to me. 'Get out.' He sparked up a cigarette before slamming the door, adjusting his braces as he marched down to greet him.

I jumped from the cab and followed them down through the yard and into the office. I hated it in there, with its stink of oil and testosterone, tatty posters of topless girls and random old car parts spread all over the rotting carpet.

They were clearly expecting me.

'Here's the champ,' smirked Uncle Tory.

My grandfather widened a sapphire eye and focused it on me like the barrel of a loaded gun. 'You feeling better, Mikey?'

I didn't open my mouth for fear of being mocked for my high voice.

'He's still a mute, then,' cackled Uncle Tory. 'What have you done to him, Frankie?'

I felt awful for my father, who was being mocked in such a cruel way because of me.

Tory and Noah were sitting on some upturned crates, leafing through old editions of the *Daily Sport*. I sat to one side of them, on a crate passed to me by Uncle Joseph, who gave me a sneaky wink and put his hand on the pit of my back. As they continued to mock, he rubbed my back as Mrs Kerr did when I was upset. Those rare moments of affection always made me tearful, but I swallowed my tears for the sake of my father's pride.

'What are we gonna do with the boy then, Frankie?' said Tory.

They discussed their plans for my week of boot camp hell as I sat quietly, determined I would win their respect and give my father some faith in me.

I looked at Tory and Noah, both perfect specimens of what young Gypsy men should be: rugged, deep-voiced, loose-limbed and great in the ring. Everything I was not.

Uncle Joseph left the office too as I was sent out to collect my father's fags from the lorry. He heaved his bulky body into the cab of his own lorry and started the engine. Before driving off he leaned out of the window. 'Just learn to switch off, Mikey. I do it all the time. You don't have to listen to them. They don't know nothing.'

Grateful for his kindness, I gave him a smile. 'I'll see you later,' I called out as he pulled away.

Back inside I endured a couple of hours of fighting talk before I could bear it no longer and went to sit in the lorry. I had smuggled Skeletor under the passenger seat. After another hour, I was called back inside to hear my fate.

I was going to travel with Uncle Tory in his lorry for the next week. Then after work each day I would be going to the boxing club, to be trained.

I didn't know which sounded worse, learning about the scrap-metal business, or training in the club. But I had no choice about either. The only thing I was looking forward to was watching the crusher in action. I wanted to see if it could really squish a car to the size of a shoebox.

Before he left, my father took me to one side and spelled out the number one rule: I must always flatter Tory when driving with him to jobs. 'Don't sit like a mute, like you do with me, ask him questions. Make him feel cushti,' he said.

That afternoon Granddad Noah and Uncle Joseph headed off to the pink caravan, while I was driven back to Tory Manor with Uncle Tory and the two boys.

I didn't like the house at all. To me, the windows and curved front door resembled the features of a contorted demonic face, while inside the front hall the lamps were in the shape of bronze demons with horns which each held a candle. Everyone said the Manor was haunted, and I found it easy to believe. I had never stayed there before, and didn't want to now.

In the vast kitchen Aunt Maudie was frying. The smell of chip fat was everywhere; she would never cook anything unless she could lower it into the vat of fat she had constantly popping away in the kitchen.

Next to her in the kitchen sat their ancient parrot. He was nearly bald, hunched like an old vulture and would imitate Maudie's long-dead mother like a morbid tape recorder.

On my first morning – which was also, as it turned out, my last – I was woken up bright and early by Aunt Maudie, who came to my room with tea, Jammy Dodgers and an omelette that looked like a large turd.

Uncle Tory was already up, having taken the boys for a 6 a.m. jog. By the time I'd swallowed what I could of my breakfast he was already in the lorry, warming it up. There was no time to wash if I wanted to keep him happy. I was just thankful that I wasn't dragged out of bed for the three-mile run. I splashed some water on my face from the outside tap that Old Noah used to use to rinse his shoes.

'Morning, champ,' said Tory as I swung open the door and climbed in.

'Morning.' My voice couldn't have sounded any squeakier. Tory looked at me, narrow-eyed. I cleared my throat and repeated myself, this time in such a deep voice that it made me choke.

The cab was huge. Looking out of the window was like standing upstairs in a two-storey house. The last time I'd been that high up was in Jamie-Leigh's *Dynasty* Wendy house, which had two storeys and a balcony, where I would stand screaming, 'Fly, my pretties, fly!'

Five minutes into the journey I still hadn't said a word. I cleared my throat again. 'So, where are we going?'

'To collect some scrap that I have to pick up.'

'Oh.'

I remembered what father said. 'Don't be a mute. Make him feel cushti.' I took a stab. 'My dad says you've met Frank Bruno.'

'Yep.'

'What's he like?'

'A cunt.'

'Oh.'

I had often heard my father bragging about the celebrities that Uncle Tory had rubbed shoulders with in his time as a boxer. Most were the usual Walsh exaggerations, but I knew it was true that Muhammad Ali had been befriended by Tory at a boxing event and had accepted an invitation to come for dinner at Tory Manor because I had seen the album, the scrapbook and the framed pictures many times: Muhammad sparring up with young Tory, Muhammad sparring up with young Noah, Muhammad sitting in the lounge, Muhammad shaking hands with Old Noah, joined at the hip – thumbs in the air – with Uncle Tory himself and standing beside a very bemused Granny Ivy. At the time she had just failed her seventh driving test and couldn't have cared less if the Pope himself had popped his head in.

'Who else have you met then?'

He paused and then started to rattle off a list of names, most of which I didn't recognise. 'So, you name a celebrity and I bet you I've met them . . . Mikey?'

I had switched off as he ploughed through his list, and was bobbing my head from side to side, along with the dancing Christmas tree hanging from the driving mirror. Now Uncle Tory was peering at me, a puzzled look on his face.

I searched my mind for any name that might impress Tory. As his stare lingered, my palms began to sweat. My father's face appeared in my head, glaring at me and mouthing names of people I could not make out through the oversized imaginary fag hanging from his lip.

The moment of truth: 'Come on then,' Uncle Tory growled. This had become a sadistic game; a puzzle that I had to solve, or die. I was trying to think of people who weren't cartoon characters or just random numbers, passing through my thoughts like pointless invaders. Then a surge of energy began to rise from my guts. One person who I would surely die to hear he had met. In my head my father began to shout, 'Someone butch, *SOMEONE BUTCH!*' My throat clogged with an excitement as, in the most frantic and completely deranged tone, I belted out, 'Oh my God, have you met Madonna?'

As I spoke the words I realised my mistake. I fell back

into the seat and threw my hands over my mouth. But it was too late. The brakes jerked for a mere second, throwing me against the dashboard. Uncle Tory's eyes had frosted over and he looked at me as if I was something he had trodden in.

'No. I haven't met' – he almost gagged just saying it – 'Madonna.'

I had blown it.

We didn't go to the job, we headed straight to the yard, where Uncle Joseph, Tory and Noah were outside chucking some tyres into a skip fire. The whole place was thick with black smoke.

Uncle Tory leaned across me and opened the passenger door.

'Get out, Mikey.' He signalled to young Tory and Noah. 'I need you boys to come with me.'

Joseph walked around to the driver's window and spoke in a polite whisper. 'Ain't you meant to be taking Mikey out with you today?'

As I clambered down the steps I watched Tory mouth the word 'useless'. I jumped the last steps and crashed to the ground, tearing my T-shirt, grazing my stomach and knocking Noah over in the process.

Uncle Tory told Joseph to phone my father and tell him to come and collect me.

As Uncle Tory and the boys drove off, Uncle Joseph stared at the blood across my stomach. 'You're bleeding,' he said.

I looked down. 'And I've ripped my T-shirt.'

He took me inside and put on the heater. 'Get that top off,' he said.

I hated my body, so I kept the T-shirt on. The bars on the heater crackled and started to glow and Uncle Joseph came back with a box of plasters and a damp piece of rag. 'You're bleeding, Mikey, take it off.'

'Can I just keep it on, it's cold.'

'Mikey, there's nothing left of the old thing now anyway.' He grabbed at my shirt and lifted it over my head, tossing it to the floor. 'Get yourself on this table.'

I used an old car engine as a stepping-stone and stood shivering on the table as he slapped the wet rag onto the wound. Compared to others I'd had it was minor. My belly jiggled as Joseph moved the rag around. 'I feel silly,' I giggled.

'It's all right,' he laughed. 'I've got a lot more than you have.' And with that, he shoved an arm under his top and cradled his stomach like a monster sack of porridge.

'Here, this'll make it better.' He lifted the old heater and placed it on the engine, aiming it at me. He manoeuvred me round in circles like a kebab on a spit, dabbing away at the excess blood.

'Are you hurting anywhere else?'

'Nope.'

'Nowhere?'

'No, I don't hurt at all.'

He put down the cloth and placed his hand just below the cut pushing his fingers into my stomach. 'How about here?'

'Nope,' I smiled proudly.

He lowered his hand and placed it behind my belt buckle. 'Here?'

I giggled. 'Nope.'

'Stop laughing,' he chuckled. He placed his hand on the opposite side and wiggled his fingers. 'Here?'

'No,' I laughed, pulling at his wrist.

He smiled, and lowered his hand. 'How about here?'

He wiggled his fingers again; I felt the tips tickle my penis.

I took his wrist with both hands and started to pull. 'Get it out,' I laughed.

He tickled my penis again, laughing.

'Why, Mikey? Does it make you feel funny?'

'Yes!' I screamed, pulling at his arm.

His laughing mouth snapped shut as he pushed me against the wall. He buried his hand deeper and softly grasped my penis, massaging it like a piece of moulding clay. His eyes narrowed. 'What kind of funny?'

I loosened my grip on his arm. 'I don't know.'

The crackle of the heater was the loudest thing in the room.

I could feel him moving his fingers back and forth. 'Can I see it?'

'Why?' I answered, beginning to feel very uncomfortable.

'I want to see what it looks like.'

I didn't know what I was supposed to say. I pursed my lips and nodded.

Uncle Joseph removed his hand and lifted my legs, slowly removing my shoes and socks, then everything else. I was naked on the table, trying to stay within the warmth of the heater's beam.

'Turn around,' said Joseph, poking me in the arm.

I did, five times or so, feeling more like a kebab than ever. He shouted me to stop as I faced the wall. I opened my eyes and stared into the cold blue paintwork resting my hands against the wall.

He moved closer, and sighed. 'Mikey, you are the prettiest boy amongst Gypsies.' He stroked a finger across my buttocks. I was scared.

'Am I?' My high-pitched squeak had returned, and made him snigger.

'Yes. Those two boys can fight, but that's because it's what they've been bred to do. What you've got cannot be learned; you've been born with what you have. One day, when you grow into it, you will make them all sick as pigs. Remember that.'

I wasn't sure exactly what he meant.

'I will, Uncle Joseph.'

'How clean are you, Mikey?'

'I got shot with the hosepipe yesterday.'

For the next hour he raped me, with every part of his body that would fit into mine.

When it was over, as I pulled my clothes back on, he pointed a finger into my face. 'Listen, Mikey, what you got me to do today, if he finds out, he will *kill* you.'

'But I didn't . . .'

He gave me a soft clip up the side of the head. 'If I tell him what happened, when he gets through this door . . .'

Through the window, behind Joseph's shoulder, my father stepped from the truck, lighting a cigarette and adjusting his braces.

'Please don't tell him!'

'I won't if you don't. Take an oath you won't talk to him about it, and I'll make up something that will make you look cushti.'

'All right!'

'Good.' He turned in his chair as my father stepped through the doorway. 'How yer doin boyeeee?'

'How are ya, Mush, all right?' my father replied with a half smile.

'Cushti, bruv, cushti.'

'I can see that.' He turned to me. 'Why ain't you out workin'?'

Joseph leaned back in his chair, locking his fingers and stretching out his arms. 'Stop talking like that to the boy, Frankie. He's been out there working with me all day.'

'Have you?' my father said, almost shocked at Joseph's positive comment.

I nodded.

'Yes he has.' Joseph repeated.

'Why didn't he go with Tory?'

'Because he was needed here! Fucking hell, Frankie, you said you wanted the boy to come here and work and that's what he's been doing.'

I stiffened, waiting to see if he would buy the story.

'And he did all right?'

'Better than all right, Frank.'

'I'll bring him back to you next week, then.'

'Yeah. You'd like that, wouldn't you, Mikey?'

I slipped down from the chair, holding on to the overalls. They both stared, waiting for my reply. I managed a smile.

'Yeah.'

10

That Evil Bowers Girl

For the next few years, I was sent to the scrapyard one day a week.

Joseph had offered to 'train' me, and Uncle Tory and my father were only too happy to leave me to him. Uncle Tory would take off in the lorry, with young Tory and Noah, and I would be left to the mercies of my uncle for hours at a time.

Every week he would take me into the back room, make me take my clothes off, and repeat the nightmare all over again. He would lift me across old Noah's desk, where I would lie on my back as he stuffed a clenched fist into my mouth while he masturbated. Just as I felt my jaw was about to break, he would pull out and fill my mouth with the sticky mess that squirted from him.

As the weeks went by he would try different experiments, painful acts that left me unable to swallow or sit or even breathe too deeply. Sometimes he would kick and punch and scratch me during these sessions. If Tory or my grandfather were in the office that day then he would take me out in the lorry; making me either strip and play with myself or go down on him as we drove to our next scrap pick up. There was no escape.

I couldn't say no. Not just because he was triple my size, but also because he had all the power. If I didn't do what he wanted he would tell my father, and we both knew that one word about me having 'played up' would get me a beating.

I did try, once, to tell my father what was happening. It was the same day that I had tried to refuse Joseph's advances. He had got his revenge by telling my father that I had been lazy and answered him back.

In the car on the way home my father lashed out at me.

'Answering Joseph back! (Thud) Being lazy! (Wham).'

I decided to tell my father everything about Joseph, and what he had done. But as I told him, falteringly, about what was happening, his eyes exploded with rage at my gruesome 'lie'. He began to shout above my pleas, then, not being able to quieten me, he slammed his fist into my mouth, splattering my lips through the gaps of my teeth. He did not want to hear it, and it only made my punishment worse. I knew then that I could never tell anyone. I was utterly alone.

I was still wetting the bed every night and being taken out to the beating shed every morning. If I had extra scratches and bruises, my father didn't notice or care.

Around the rest of the family Joseph acted as though we were friends who shared a secret; winking, joking and acting as though my silence meant I liked the things he did.

I was trapped. But it wasn't Joseph that I feared most. It was what my father would do if I didn't do as Joseph said. As long as I played the game, Joseph told my father I had worked hard and done well. That's how it worked.

At the campsite Frankie and I were no longer alone. As more plots were completed, more families arrived, and we children became an inseparable clan. A year after we first moved in the site was finished and it seemed we had finally settled somewhere that we could stay.

Coming back to the camp from anywhere else was like entering into another world: a full-scale exotic trailer-filled town, created and built by Gypsies for Gypsies. Fresh concrete had been poured on top of the mud that had once been everywhere, and a smart road of jet-black tarmac flowed right through it. At the main entrance the walls curved and spiralled ingeniously like frozen waves. At the very tip of each solid wave stood the life-sized stone head of a wild horse, peering like a milky-eyed guardian at the people passing below. And inside, the plots were no longer marked out with red string, but with scarlet brick walls, eight feet tall, surrounding each home like gigantic theatrical curtains.

We were still at St Luke's School, with Jamie-Leigh Bowers, our cousins Olive and Twizzel and a few of the other children from the site. None of the other kids liked school, and I pretended not to, but secretly I needed it as a refuge; it kept me from being at home, or with Joseph.

Our parents saw school as a place where we had to go, because the law said so, and they didn't care whether we learned anything there. My mother was the exception, she wanted me to read and write, and so did Mrs Kerr, who encouraged me and tried to help, whenever I was in her class.

Ever since the accident in class and the knickers moment, she had fought my corner and encouraged my artistic skills, and she stuck up for me when the school bully, Scott Leemer, had a go at me. She even gave me a wink when we were taken to the Head's office for a telling off.

I came to love Mrs Kerr. She was the only person who showed me tenderness and affection. To have one person believe in me and encourage me to be whatever I wanted to be was the most wonderful thing that ever happened to me.

My education was patchy, to say the least, but I did manage to learn the alphabet well enough to recognise the look and sound of each letter, and to read and write a few three-letter words: dog, cat, run. But most of all I enjoyed art. Drawing people fascinated me and I could do a good pencil portrait.

I wished I could go to school every day, but although I was supposed to go four days a week, it often ended up being just one or two. I would be given jobs about the plot, or sent to the scrapyard for an extra day, while the girls were kept back and trained in how to run a home.

When we did get to school we were either ignored or picked on by the other kids. Only lunchtime gave us a break, because we had our own dinner table. No one else dared to sit there, in case they found themselves cursed, robbed blind or with some kind of monstrous Pikey disease.

When it came to the staff Mrs Kerr was in a minority of one. Even the dinner ladies hated us. Every day they made sure we were the last to be asked to queue for food, which meant we only got what was left by all the other kids. The ladies behind the counter would glare as they slapped the dried-up remains onto our plates. A slice of spam fritter, without the fritter, was a rare treat.

Mrs Bannerman was the head dinner lady. We called her Old Pig's Head and it suited her. She had a dyed orange comb-over and a permanently sour face.

One lunchtime Jamie-Leigh and Olive and Twizzel returned from the queue. Twizzel was cackling and pointing at Olive's tray. 'You got a feather up your arse?' said Frankie, drowning her food in tomato sauce.

'Look what dat old cunt's just give me ferr me dinner.'

We leaned over to look at what looked scarily like a chain-smoker's lung. Olive picked up a fork and prodded the black lump, which sank to the plate like a melting witch. 'Old piggy wotsit made her have it!'

We opened up our yogurt cartons, licking the lids and discussing where we would play after school. Frankie wanted to venture out of our camp to explore the grounds of the mental home next door.

She aimed her empty yogurt pot at me like a cannon. 'You have to as well, Mikey. If I get killed by me dad, then I ain't going through it on my own.'

'I wanted to go anyway,' I insisted.

Cheers of agreement flew around the table.

Then Mrs Bannerman appeared. 'Just *what* is all this commotion about?'

'Nothing,' replied Twizzel, narrowing her eyes.

'Good. Then pick up that cutlery and eat your food. That's if you are accustomed to using cutlery.' She glared at us, before marching away.

'Old cunt,' said Jamie-Leigh through her teeth, dropping a spoon into her yogurt pot. She pulled in her cheeks making a digging sound in her throat and spat a slug of rubbery green slime into her yogurt pot.

'Miss, this yogurt's gone off.'

Old Pig's Head turned and came back to the table. She snatched the pot from Jamie-Leigh's hand and picked up a clean spoon, then stirred slowly through the mush before raising a loaded spoonful to her mouth.

'Tastes fine to me, Miss Bowers. Maybe next time you won't be so fussy.'

She stalked off, as we cried with laughter.

At playtime we would all meet in the girls' toilet so that the girls could grab a sly after lunch cigarette – most of them, including Frankie, were experienced smokers by the age of ten.

One break time Olive, our nominated look-out that day, was spotted by Mrs Bannerman, who gave chase. Olive raced into the girls' toilets to warn us, slamming the door open so hard that it smashed into Jamie-Leigh's front teeth. Jamie-Leigh's head flew back, blood all over her mouth. She put her arm into her mouth to stop herself screaming and leaned against the door. Seconds later Mrs Bannerman barged through the door.

'Aaargh! My tooth.'

I stood, slack-jawed and in total awe of Jamie-Leigh's deviousness.

'You spiteful old witch. Look what you've done!' she sobbed.

Mrs Bannerman fell back against the wall in shock; her hands flew to her mouth as she peered around the side of the door to where Jamie-Leigh was cupping a tooth in a small pool of blood in her hand. The blood trickled between her fingers and down her arms. At that point two other dinner ladies came in, giving Mrs Bannerman disapproving looks, as they escorted Jamie-Leigh off to the nurse.

When we took our seats on the carpet in Mrs Kerr's classroom that afternoon, Jamie-Leigh was still with the nurse, waiting for her mother to come and collect her. The school assistant came in to warn Mrs Kerr that she had arrived.

Seconds later the sound of Aunt Audrey's stiletto heels echoed through the school. She swung into our classroom, tossing her black hair and throwing her mink stole over her shoulder. She was wearing more diamonds than clothes, which was typical for her. She eyed Mrs Kerr like a cobra. 'Where's my Jamie-Leigh?'

Mrs Kerr rose from her seat. 'Oh, hello Mrs Bowers.'

'Oh, fuck off will you,' Aunt Audrey snapped. She had an accent that sounded like a fork dragging across a plate.

Mrs Kerr tried to edge her out of the room, but at that moment Aunt Audrey spotted us on the carpet. 'Hiya kids!' she squealed, waving a heavily bejewelled hand.

Mrs Kerr took Aunt Audrey to where Jamie-Leigh was, before coming back to take her seat for register. She had to raise her voice to drown out the profanities ringing through the school corridors, as Aunt Audrey saw the damage to her child.

After that the teachers banned us from going indoors during breaks, so we moved our lunchtime rendezvous to a small brick maze which was hidden from the school playground and had plenty of nooks to hide – and smoke – in.

We kept ourselves to ourselves because more often than not our contact with the Gorgia kids ended in an exchange of taunts, insults and scraps. And sometimes fully fledged fights broke out. The girls were almost always the main targets of the prejudice. And they could never let a bad comment go. No matter how big, ugly or threatening the bully, our girls would never back down from a fight.

A lot of nasty comments were aimed at me, but as long as the girls weren't around to hear it, I would turn a deaf ear. But when the girls were involved and things became heated, I would be called on to step in and defend their honour. It was my duty as the boy. I hated violence; I couldn't stand it. But I could never seem to escape it. At home, at work, and now even at school, there was always someone who wanted to beat me up.

There was an important lesson I had been taught about fighting, and strangely it had not come from my father, but from my mother.

'Never throw a punch. Never be a bully. Never go looking for a fight. But if anyone ever hits you and it hurts, then they deserve to be hit back.'

I tried to stick to this. And on those occasions when I did have to hit back, I had one big advantage – what the little monsters who bullied us didn't know, was that my tolerance for physical pain was far higher than theirs.

I soon discovered that most of those I had to fight were just a lot of hot air. They bullied anyone who showed fear, but if you fought back, they turned out to be cowards.

The number one bully at the school was Scott Leemer. Most of the kids either admired him for his quiff, like Danny Zuko from *Grease*, and his thuggish ways, or steered clear of the gang of little thugs he headed. His right-hand man was Jenny Hardy. A girl in name only, almost as feared and loathed by most of us as Scott was.

One playtime I arrived at the maze to find them waiting for me. The gang, who were all older than me, surrounded me and began to close in. Then Scott walked in, handed his jacket to another kid, and began leaping around, bashing his fists together like a cartoon boxer.

I thought he looked pathetic compared to the boys at the boxing club.

He threw some pretend punches to make me flinch. 'I hear you're hard, Gypsy boy.'

He walked up to me and pushed me with both hands, and I fell over. A crowd was gathering around us. I spotted the girls, peering through the crowd, each looking a little worse for wear. Frankie's face was red and tear-stained and her lip was bleeding. Her pretty pigtails had been yanked about and undone.

'Kill him!' she screamed.

I looked over at Scott, who was circling with his arms in the air, working the crowd like a pro. 'Shall I do it?' He was laughing.

They howled and screeched, shaking their fists in a primal excitement, hungry for Gypsy blood.

Above the noise, I could hear the girls, screaming 'Kill him, Mikey, kill him.'

As the only Gypsy boy in school, I knew I was sworn to fight for the girls, and for the honour of our culture, no matter what. Scott was much bigger than me. My heart was pounding and my mouth felt dry. But one thought, above all others, stood out in my mind: if I lose, my father will surely find out about it. And a bashing from this boy would be nothing to what I would get from him.

Suddenly I saw red. I imagined I was back in the ring with Paddy, the crowd shouting and cheering around us. At that moment Scott's first two punches landed on me.

Winded, I doubled over. He stood back, taunting and jeering and running around the circle doing high fives. A tear slid down my cheek.

The crowd started to chant. 'Gypos go home, Gypos go home!'

Scott turned back to finish me off. I looked round and saw Frankie, Olive and Twizzel being pinned down by some of the bigger boys, as several other boys held a raging Jamie-Leigh while Jenny Hardy threw punches at her face.

I turned back to Scott, who was laughing. He raised his fists, and so did I. We circled one another, before he kissed his fist and went in for a punch. The chorus swelled as he turned back to finish me off.

'You stinking . . . Gypsy . . . bastards; coming here and ruining our school. You make me sick.' He hit me square in the stomach. Bent towards me he gave me a perfect opportunity. I grabbed his mane of hair and locked my fists there.

The crowd started to groan, as Scott screamed and fell to his knees, shouting and trying to grab my arms. He dug his nails into my fingers, but I wasn't letting go.

I saw my father's yellow eyes and felt the sting of his bamboo cane falling on my skin. I thought of Joseph, groaning with pleasure, not caring about the pain and fear he inflicted on me.

With strength I didn't know I had, I lifted him off the ground and began to swing him round by his hair, faster and faster, in a dizzying circle. He was screaming at the top of his voice and I could feel his scalp was bleeding, but nothing was going to stop me now. Fury surged through me and I swung him until tufts of his hair came out in my hands and he flew backwards into the horrified crowd.

As they parted and then ran for cover, Jenny Hardy ran towards me, her face contorted with rage. I drew back my fist and launched it into her chest, sending her hurtling to the floor. As she landed, Jamie-Leigh, Frankie and the other two girls pounced, tearing wildly at her face, hair, clothes and body like a pack of furious she-wolves.

Scott was sitting on the ground, sobbing, a clump of his hair in his hand. 'Look what you've done to me,' he shouted. I walked away. I was trembling with the effort of what I'd done. But I felt exhilarated. Then the dinner ladies pounced, and we were all sent to the headmaster's office.

Judging by its compact size, Mr Wadsworth's office had not catered for so many misbehaving children at once. Of course we Gypsies had been there before. In fact we knew his office as well as we knew our classrooms; we appeared there most days for some misdemeanour or other.

Sitting in the corner was Dotty Quinlan, a girl rumoured to have been struck by lightning, and always in trouble because of her fondness for painting with faeces. She was sitting in her usual seat, knees tightly together and dressed in a Dorothy pinafore, with enormous spectacles and a haircut like a thatched cottage. She never spoke to us; she just buried her head beneath the neck of her dress like an old tortoise.

Mr Wadsworth was in such a fury he had completely lost the ability to speak an audible sentence. As he stood behind his desk, shouting, the only part I could hear clearly was the '*Do you understand*?' bit at the end.

At that point, Jamie-Leigh chose to release a colossal

fart into the room. She laughed out loud, showing off her new, pointy front teeth, as the impact ricocheted off the base of her chair. Laughter spread throughout the room and Mr Wadsworth cupped his head in his hands as we wiped tears from our hysterical faces.

It was clear that our headmaster had come to the end of his tether with the battle of Gorgias versus Gypsies. It was never going to be resolved. No matter how well we Gypsy children behaved, no matter how much we tried to stay out of trouble, there would always be someone wanting to have a go at us, and being proud of who we were, we could never let it go.

11

Kevin

One day Tyrone Donoghue came home with a young homeless man he had spotted outside Harrods, the posh department store in London. Gypsies and Travellers often pick up their workmen – known as dossas – from the streets of big cities, most commonly London, and take them home to help with their general chores and any kind of dodgy deed they may be plotting. A homeless man can't refuse if someone carrying Harrods bags offers him a place to stay and money in his pocket every week.

So Kevin was ushered into the back of Tyrone Donoghue's van and brought back to Warren Woods.

The dread on his face was even clearer than the dirt on it when he stepped out of the vehicle and saw all of us staring back at him as if he was an alien. And that's exactly what he was. A tall, gangly boy, his hair combed into a neat side-parting and wearing clothes that were too small for him, he wasn't a Gypsy like us, which put him into a different world instantly. And he was soon made very aware of how inhumane the travellers of Mr Donoghue's kind were to a mere Gorgia man. Dossas were considered beneath both Gypsies and Travellers, and were generally despised. But Mr Donoghue took their treatment to a new low with his cruelty towards Kevin.

In a matter of days, Kevin was sleeping in the back of

the van that had brought him and was being terrorised daily by Mr Donoghue, his wife and five children. Scared of saying no or of standing up to their cruel demands, Kevin spent twelve hours a day painting, washing cars, walking and feeding fierce dogs, shovelling bricks, cement, dirt and mortar, laying tarmac single handed and even towing the Donoghue children around on a cart like a Shire horse.

He never refused, but he was still beaten regularly. Mr Donoghue would punch him just because he'd had a bad day at work. The children pelted him with stones and Mrs Donoghue refused to have him eat off her own plates and gave him one of the dogs' dishes.

My father, being a friend and regular pub-going accomplice of Mr Donoghue, regularly witnessed the terrible life Kevin led at the hands of the Donoghue clan.

One day, sick of his modest tool shed, and in need of a helping hand to put up a bigger one, my father asked Mr Donoghue if he could borrow Kevin for a morning.

'Of course, Frank, and if he gives you any trouble, or don't shift his weight for you, drag him back up here to me,' Mr Donoghue said.

Once Kevin was out of sight of his owner, he broke down, pleading to my father to save him. 'I'll work for you for nothing, Frank. Please help me.'

'I'll try, my boy. I'll try,' whispered my father.

He gave him a pat on the back, threw me a stiff glance and they both went about their work.

I stared after them, astonished. It seemed that Kevin had somehow got through to my unmerciful and cruel father. Sure enough, that evening down at the pub, my father dosed Mr Donoghue with whisky and made him an offer of a hundred pounds for Kevin to work for him instead. Mr Donoghue gave in and they shook on it.

They spent the hundred pounds in the next hour, and Frankie and I awoke the next morning to find Kevin cleaning our window. We both gave him a wave. He waved back, and despite his bruises and a thick lip, he had a beaming smile that lit up his face.

The new tool shed, known as the stable, became home for Kevin. My mother bought him a bed and a dresser as well as a fridge, a cooker and a lamp powered by a huge cable extension that ran from our electric box. He quickly became one of the family. My father even took him to buy a brand-new wardrobe and have a haircut, and he promised him a decent wage, so that he could save up and get a life outside work. And away from us.

My father had saved Kevin, and yet at the same time Kevin had saved my father. Kevin's innocence and need for help awoke a side of my father that we had never seen before. For the first time in his life, there was someone who didn't look on him as a monster. He was a hero. And he clearly enjoyed every living, breathing moment of being one.

Two joyous weeks went by. Then my father bought Kevin a TV and Kevin climbed onto the stable roof to set up the aerial.

That afternoon Frankie and I were running around the plot with Olive, Twizzel and Jamie-Leigh, playing a game called 'He loves a Bitta Girl', which was basically a kissing version of tag.

Right in the middle of a clinch, there was a sudden explosion of fireworks, followed by a hissing and crackling and Kevin tumbled down from the stable roof and crashed at our feet. His body hit the concrete paving, heaving an out breath of clear smoke, and the smell of burning meat filled the air. We didn't know it then, but Kevin had touched the electric cable that ran above the shed, with his aerial.

After a couple of seconds of utter shock, we ran and told my mother and then Jamie-Leigh and I ran for the neighbours, banging on doors and shouting for help.

It took an ambulance forty-five minutes to come to Kevin's aid.

He hadn't a hope.

We children were left deeply shocked. Kevin had been carried into the air and slammed to the ground by a force we'd had no idea existed. Watching our friend die in front of us was something we could never understand or forget. Whenever Olive, Twizzel, Jamie-Leigh, Frankie and I were together, we talked about it for many years afterwards.

The day after the accident, my mother, Henry-Joe, Frankie and I were cleaning out Kevin's room, when my mother came across a letter. As she read it she started to cry. She sat on his bed and laid Henry-Joe beside her. It was a birthday card, addressed to Kevin's mother.

A guilt-ridden Mr Donoghue and my father paid for a lovely funeral for Kevin. The mourners were us, the Donoghue family and, to our surprise, Kevin's mum.

I can still hear her voice, and her words of unconditional love for her only son and the one word she kept repeating: sorry. For what, we'll never know.

12

The Monster in the Woods

My eighth birthday fell on a Saturday, which meant no school, and no father till evening, as he was off working. We didn't have birthday parties, but we didn't need them, there were always friends to play with and for me just being free for the day was enough. I didn't expect presents, girls got presents and a cake, boys just got a bit of money.

Frankie and I were playing in her battered Wendy house with the other girls when Sadie popped up over the wall from the plot next door. Sadie was a boy and, like me, was born into a family of fighters. His father, impressed by the Johnny Cash song 'A Boy Named Sue', about a boy who grew up to be a fighter because of his stupid name, thought he would try the same ploy with his own son.

Unfortunately it backfired totally, because Sadie turned out to be the most camp Gypsy boy ever to set foot in a caravan. When his father realised that not only would he never make a fighter, but that he was not going to match the description of a Gypsy man in any respect whatsoever, he was horrified. He banned Sadie from setting foot outside their caravan, so that no one would set eyes on him.

By the time he was in his mid-teens Sadie had the voice, hairstyle, mannerisms, wardrobe, and even the figure, of a voluptuous silver-screen siren. When his father was out, he would venture out of the caravan and as far as the wall dividing our plot from his, where he would climb on the electric box next to the wall and poke his head over, in the hope of finding someone to talk to. His hair always arrived before he did. He had the most amazing bouffant hair-do we had ever seen, and he flaunted it with obvious delight. It would appear over the wall, followed by Sadie's heavily made-up face.

He would lie in wait for my mother, who went out daily to sweep her beloved crazy paving, which by this time covered the whole of our plot. She didn't mind Sadie, but after a while she got fed up with the constant interruptions and started to wait until his father was at home before going out to sweep, knowing that Sadie wouldn't be allowed to come out.

Undaunted, Sadie turned to us children for company. He would watch from the window until we went out to play, and then appear over the wall and chat to us as we played. He must have been very lonely, though we didn't think about it then.

When he appeared on my birthday we hadn't seen him for a week or two.

'Hiya guys! Have you missed me?' he drawled in a fake American accent.

'It's Mikey's birthday today, Sadie.'

'Ooohh, is it? How old are you?'

Frankie, crawling around the front gate with her bottom in the air, responded for me. 'He's eight.'

'It was mine the other week – I was seventeen,' beamed Sadie. 'What are you doing for it?'

'I'm going spider hunting,' I told him.

'What did you do for yours?' asked Jamie-Leigh, pulling the last legs from her prey.

'Me mum paid for me to go to America with me aunt Julie – you wanna see some pictures?'

'Yeah, go on then.'

Sadie's face glowed. 'I'll be right back.'

Before we could escape he was back and he hoisted himself over the wall. He was wearing a pair of beige, skin-tight flares and holding a large, red and pink fabric covered book with SADIE glued on the front in blue sequins.

While we stood around trying to look interested, he flicked through pages, each one beautifully decorated and filled with photos of his holiday, most of them close-ups of him, framed against the Disneyland castle. He told the story of every picture until we'd had enough of being polite and ran off to play.

Sadie came out to speak to us most days. And even when he was locked away and couldn't come out, he would open his window, blasting tracks from his latest albums, miming the words and striking various poses at the window.

The camp's behaviour toward Sadie was, unsurprisingly, never kind. He was a victim of relentless verbal abuse and name-calling. He was mocked and jeered, especially by the men, and his father made no secret of his shame. For years Sadie's name was used by many as a term of insult toward anyone with his kind of 'ways'. Yet despite it all, Sadie refused to change for an easier life. He was who he was, and that was that. And though I never would have dared to say it, I admired Sadie, who in his own way was just as brave as any other man on the site.

*   *   *

Two months after my birthday my mother was taken into
hospital and she arrived home a week later with a baby
with silky skin and eyes just like my father's: wide, black,
shiny stones full of nothing. I peered into his cot one
morning and watched him as he cried. I reached for the
bottle of milk and placed it by his mouth. He suckled
quietly, clenching his fists, as I stared down at him: I knew
this was the one. This was who I should have been: the
boy who would be a fighter and make my father proud.

When my parents came in and saw me with him they
went berserk. I was unworthy even to stand near to him.
My father lifted me by the hair and threw me from the
bedroom and slammed the door in my face.

Jimmy. A Walsh through and through.

All my father's hopes now rested on his new son. He
had given up on making a true fighter of me, and Henry-
Joe was my mother's son, protected and mollycoddled,
but Jimmy would be a champion. None of us doubted it.

Despite this, I was still dragged weekly to the boxing
club, forced to go through my paces, and made to suffer
whatever humiliations my father could put my way.

Every week I would be weighed, and then put through
a hardcore exercise routine of sit-ups, push-ups, pull-ups
– on an old doorframe – skipping, hitting the punch bag
and then sparring with Uncle Tory, who would hold up
pads with a little red spot on each, and make me hit them
as fast and as many times as I could.

Despite my loathing of the whole business, I did grow
physically fit. Not to the standards of Tory and Noah, but
I could see it in the difference between me and the majority
of other boys at the boxing club. They may have been put

through their paces, but they weren't doing half the work there that I was being asked to do. I hated to admit it and I never did to them, but when I was on those punch bags, I could vent the anger inside of me. It only helped more to have Uncle Joseph constantly looking over my shoulder, or Uncle Tory's face in between those punching mitts. Every strike to that bag was another blow to them.

My stomach grew solid and my legs, like a football player's. But in the opinion of the Walsh men, being physically fit didn't mean that I was able to fight. After the calamity of my first fight, my father, uncle and grandfather had decided I would not fight again until I reached the age of twelve – the age of manhood to Gypsies – and for this at least I was grateful. When the boxing matches started, the three of them would join the other men around the ring. Uncle Tory told me I couldn't afford the time to be in the audience, so I was sent outside to spar with my cousin, young Noah.

By this time Noah had decided he wasn't too keen on boxing. He was fourteen and more interested in where he was going with his friends afterwards. They would all go into the local town to look for Gorgia women to score with. So when the coast was clear Noah and I would put down our gloves and stand together outside, sharing our hatred of boxing.

In between school, chores, the boxing club and the scrapyard, there wasn't a lot of free time. But when there was, I loved to take off on a bike. No child on the camp had ever been bought a bike to fit. Most of us rattled round on one that was several sizes too big. We managed to ride them all right, but stopping was a bit of a problem.

Slamming the brakes on guaranteed a swift flight over the handlebars.

Frankie, Olive and Jamie-Leigh had perfected the knack of jumping off, letting the bike carry on to a natural stop against the nearest wall.

Twizzel and I, however, being younger, had not yet managed to master the knack of jumping off. But we'd discovered that crashing into a fence usually did just as well.

My father's friend Mike had set up his own business, stealing bikes by the truckload from the local sports centre and selling them at random Sunday markets. The kids of the camp were his guinea pigs; he gave us the task of test-riding each bike and giving our opinion on each one's condition and saleability. Not only did we get to ride the bikes, but he paid us a fiver a week, which we split. We couldn't believe our luck.

The tarmac road into the camp was over a mile long, so for a good while we used that. But after a while we decided to explore what lay beyond our camp.

To the east and the west were forbidden zones. On the east side stood a rotting piece of land, empty apart from a lone trailer which had been half swallowed up by the base of a huge old oak that looked like a clawed hand.

A woman whom we were convinced was a witch lived within its decomposing walls with ten black hellhounds. She had lived there quite peacefully until we Gypsies arrived. An outcast herself, she held nothing but contempt for us, setting her dogs onto anyone who dared come near her home. And those beasts aimed to hurt.

So we turned to the west, where, beyond the sewer river,

there was another secluded society: a home for people with severe mental illnesses. The patients were allowed to roam free, but only within the electrified walls that surrounded it. It was called Oak Place, and it lay deeply buried within the west woods, hidden away from the rest of the world. We all agreed that it had to be investigated and one evening, after wolfing down our dinner, we leaped upon our stolen bikes and headed out to meet the others at the one deserted plot in our camp. When we got there the troops were already assembled and Dolly and Colleen, the Donoghue sisters, were passing around a cigarette from a pack they had stolen from their mother.

Jamie-Leigh sucked back the smoke like a pro and blew it out through her nostrils. Frankie jumped from her bike, leaving it to collide with a pile of rubble, and headed towards Jamie-Leigh with her arm extended. I crashed onto the rubble pile and clambered off to head over to the group.

Frankie was taking a long drag on the cigarette, her eyes blissfully closed, as if it were the fruit of life. 'Don't tell me Dad,' she warned me. As if I would. Going on eleven, she was now a seasoned smoker, along with her fellow ten-year-olds. The four girls passed the cigarette around, reverently, while Olive and Twizzel appeared, running down the lane holding hands, looking identical in blood-red dress coats.

'Save me a bit of that,' Olive yelled.

Tagging behind them was the new recruit and only other boy of the group, Horace. Lucky enough to have completely escaped the notice of the school board, he spent most days indoors stuffing himself with sweets and watching action movies.

Horace's face was a mask of freckles and his hair was a bright red mass of straw. His parents, Aunt June and Uncle Horace, were both black-haired and olive-skinned.

Shunned by everyone but her devoted husband, Aunt June spent most days adding more hot pink to the decor of her trailer or soaping down the car in a strapless bikini and high heels.

Her strange tastes were also reflected in young Horace's wardrobe. She filled it with nothing but shell suits and Jockey boots; today's was lime green, with a hot pink stripe through the chest.

'Right,' sucked Colleen as she inhaled smoke. She crammed a double drag from the last of the filter before stubbing it out. 'Let's go.'

Dolly, being the tallest went over the wall first, to help the rest of us break our fall. From our side it was an easy climb, but the drop on the other appeared considerably longer. Dolly clambered over, rolling like a log onto the verge below before getting down onto all fours beside the wall. 'Break my back and you're dead,' she called up.

The rest of us, apart from Jamie-Leigh who jumped clear over, landing in a frog squat on the other side, climbed over and slowly lowered ourselves down, using Dolly's broad back as a stepping-stone.

Once we were all over, we made our way through the wood, ducking and diving through cobwebs and stray branches that whipped us in the face.

'Has anybody ever seen *Predator*?' asked Horace.

'Oh for goodness sake shut up, I'm scared enough as it is,' said Dolly, who was leading the way.

Twizzel, Horace and I were trailing along at the back.

'What's it about?' asked Twizzel.

'Well, it's this alien, right, and he lives in the woods or something, and he's killing all these men and pulling their heads off and stuff . . .'

We sang, cursed, fought and giggled our way deeper into the darkening forest, until the narrow path suddenly opened up into a clearing.

The girls dug out Colleen's cigarettes and lit up.

'Where are we?' Twizzel hissed.

We appeared to have stumbled upon an old campsite. In the centre was a dead campfire, with an empty barrel lying across it. Around it were three large logs, arranged as a seating area.

Jamie-Leigh grabbed Frankie's hand and edged closer to see what was inside the barrel. She peered inside, then leaped backwards. 'Oh my God,' she cried. 'There's a dead man's arm in there.'

Frankie stepped forward to have a peek. 'It's a squirrel you fool.'

We rushed over for a look. What lay there was so decomposed it could have been anything from a dog to a large rat. But on balance it looked as though Frankie was right, it was a squirrel that must have got into the barrel and become trapped.

We looked around. There was no longer just one path to take; we were surrounded by six dark dirt paths, each one as ominous and frightening as the next.

'How do we know which one we arrived on?' whimpered Colleen.

That was easy. Dolly had stopped to go to the loo and had deposited a neat pile of turds at the entrance to the path. Twizzel, Horace and I had been peering down another of the paths. In the distance we could see what looked like a large house that had sunk into the trees. Twizzel pointed. 'Let's go down this one.'

The rest of the group walked over.

'I ain't going over there,' Dolly said with a shudder.

'Fair enough, come on, leave old scaredy-crotch here,' said Frankie, linking arms with Jamie-Leigh. They began to skip down the track.

Dolly and Colleen planted themselves on one of the logs by the campfire. Dolly broke off a stick, poking it through the bars at the dead squirrel. 'I ain't going in there. We'll stay here and give him a burial.'

The rest of us turned and followed Frankie and Jamie-Leigh. As we linked arms and headed down the dark path, a thrill of fear and anticipation shot through me.

Twizzel chuckled and began chanting, 'Lions and tigers and bears, oh my!'

'Shut up!' Olive scowled, yanking Twizzel's pigtail.

When we reached the building we had seen we discovered it wasn't a house, it was an open-sided hay barn. But it had clearly not been used for some time. The few bails that were left were torn open and drooping toward the ground. Frankie and Jamie-Leigh were nowhere in sight.

'Very funny, girls,' Olive called out. 'Come on, the others want to go home.'

There was silence. A flock of crows flew over us, cawing loudly.

'This ain't funny any more, you two,' shouted Olive.

'I think we should just leave them here and go home,' said Twizzel.

'What if something's really happened to them?' I said. I was beginning to feel scared, and Horace was clinging to my arm.

Twizzel gave me a poke in the ribs. 'Like what, Mikey? Were they killed by a monster?'

'Or the Predator,' Horace added.

'Oh shut up, carrot-top, there's no such thing. Olive, come back here, now. I'm going home.'

Olive was kicking through the hay bales, swearing and cursing. The static from her coat attracted the hay like a magnet; she was beginning to look like a scarecrow. The more she brushed at herself, the more it stuck. '*I know you're in here*,' she shouted. Her voice rebounded from the shelter's ceiling and threw out a thunderous echo.

As it died out there was a moment of silence. Then a sudden snap of breaking stick had us screaming like harpies. I looked over at Olive. She was still under the shelter, standing frozen, looking back at the three of us in horror. Jamie-Leigh and Frankie leaped out from behind the barn, throwing a pile of straw over Olive. But she remained petrified. The other two girls followed her gaze, and froze too.

'Will you stop it,' said Twizzel. 'What the fuck are you doing?'

Suddenly, a voice from behind us said, 'Eoghc DErrgh Thfhhuck Err Yuuu Gdoooin?'

It was the same question, only spoken in a strange slur.

We turned to see a slobbering man, with a lop-sided face and stooping shoulders.

My throat filled with ice. None of us dared move.

The man raised the working side of his face into a rotten-toothed smile and stood swaying to and fro like a gruesome marionette. Then he hobbled forward, reached out with a limp hand and brushed it against Horace's cheek.

Suddenly his expression changed to a grimace and he grabbed Horace with both his bony hands, tightening them around his neck. Horace croaked and squealed, trying to pull at the man's large hands. But the man started to shake him violently, while howling from the back of his throat.

We sprang into action. Twizzel and I tore at his hands, as the other three ran over and kicked and punched at his legs. When we prised the man off, Horace dropped to the floor in a heap. Grabbing hold of him we started to run and sprinted back down the path to the campfire.

Dolly and Colleen were smoking cigarettes and poking at the squirrel, which by now was sprawled out on the ground.

'*Run!*' screamed Jamie-Leigh, heading back down the path towards the wall.

We arrived back in the camp, swearing never to set foot in the wood ever again.

As we approached our plot, Frankie and I could hear the sound of my father's whistle. It was a Tuesday, my evening for training at the boxing club. I prayed that he hadn't been waiting for us for too long.

When we arrived at the plot, our father was standing beside the car with a strip of bamboo in his hand. 'I've been whistling you for an hour.'

'Sorry, Dad.'

'Where have you been?'

'We climbed over the gate, over at the spare plot.'

He marched towards us, raising the bamboo above his

head. Frankie leaped clear and darted towards her Wendy house.

'You went over to the divvy home, didn't you?'

'No!'

He lashed out, catching me across the back of my legs. The pain felt like boiling water across my calves. I rolled on the ground, screaming and holding my legs in pain as he took another swipe. Then another. And another and another.

His face looked red, the veins standing out like lumps across his forehead, as he swiped at me. My whole body felt filled with scorching pain as the bamboo slashed across my arms, legs, fingers, back and face.

I knew he was angrier about me being late for the club than us going to Oak Place.

He stopped, panting, and told me to get up. I was in so much pain I couldn't move. He dropped the stick to the floor, and put me under his arm. I cried as he swore. He dragged me over to the stable and kicked me hard and square, launching me from the ground like a football. I crashed amongst the laundry as he slammed the door behind me.

'You want a dog's life, do you, my boy?' He pulled the bar across the door. 'Then I will give you one.'

Frankie came running for the door, shaking at the lock.

'Open that door and I'll kill him.'

She backed away from the door, leaving me in silence.

It was pitch dark. I sat on the floor. I could smell freshly washed and dried clothes. It was a nice smell. My father often locked me in here. He probably thought that being locked in this dark place would scare me, as it had scared him when his father locked him up as a small boy. But unlike him, I wasn't afraid of the dark. I felt calm, as I looked at the dust particles floating in the few tiny rays of light filtering through the walls and door.

I crawled over to the dryer, which was rumbling away in one corner, and leaned against it. It rumbled through the lashes on my back, soothing and comforting me.

As night drew in, the light switch outside was flicked on, the bar was pulled from the door and my mother came in, a basket of laundry in one hand and the other supporting Henry-Joe, who had his arms wrapped around her neck.

'Just what are you doing in here, shit trousers?' she joked. 'I thought you'd gone with your dad to the club.'

I hoisted myself up. 'Nah, he locked me in here instead.'

'Oh well,' she laughed, 'you're probably better off in here anyway.'

She crouched before the dryer, putting the loaded basket down beside her. Henry-Joe dived into the clothes pile, rolling blissfully around. She caught a glimpse of my face. 'What's happened to you?' she exclaimed, rising to her feet. She grabbed me under the chin, moving my face from side to side, then lifted my jumper. The welts from the bamboo stood out across my skin like angry veins. She began to curse.

'Fucking old cunt. How does he expect me to get you to school looking like that?'

'Will I have to stay home?'

'What? *No,*' she said. 'It's the only place I can put you out of sight of the old fool.'

13

Fate of the Munchkin Queen

Granddad Noah was coming out of hospital and we were all going over to Tory Manor in the evening to celebrate his return. He'd been breathless and ill for some months, and in the end he'd needed a heart bypass.

That afternoon Frankie and I set off to show a disbelieving Dolly and Colleen the Haystack Man's home and the spot on which Horace almost breathed his last. We had come well prepared, having filled several carrier bags with pinecones and rocks, but there was no sign of the monster.

Disappointed, we turned back and took another of the six paths from the clearing, which led us to Oak Place itself.

We were shocked to find that what we had thought of as a prison for mental patients was just like a quaint little village; from outside we could see thatched cottages, stables with friendly donkeys and even an all-day disco. Walking round the perimeter fence we followed the sound of cheesy pop to a huge hall, with an open front, where we could see several deranged people jumping around and throwing themselves into break dances to Michael Jackson's 'Beat It'.

It was a unanimous vote that we should all go and join in, and we managed to slip through the gate without being noticed. It wasn't until we'd had an hour or so of non-stop pop fun that we were finally escorted off the premises by four hefty, shaven-headed women guards, carrying truncheons.

We ran out through the main gates, out of breath and screaming with laughter. But as we reached the camp we heard my father whistling for us and realised that we'd been out too long.

We climbed back over the wall to find him standing there, heaving like an angry bull, and holding the dreaded bamboo stick. Frankie made the first run for it. She tried to dodge, but he managed to whip the bamboo stick across her rear end as she ran. She kept on going, holding onto her backside with both hands as she headed, screaming, towards our plot.

I tried to do the same, but as I swerved by him I tripped and landed right at his feet. Like a chicken in a fox's jaws, I played dead, hanging limp in his arms as he dragged me back to the beating shed where he whipped me ferociously with the stick, before shoving me into the truck with our mother, Frankie, Henry-Joe and Jimmy.

As we drove up the lane towards Tory Manor we saw that every tree had been tied with balloons, yellow ribbons, and misspelled signs reading, 'WELKOM BAK'.

Frankie and I had been made to feel guilty for the whole journey, and the sight of the decorations brought forth a fresh burst from our father, who gazed at them, tears in his eyes, and ranted at us about how shameful it was not to have been here early enough to help put them up.

'It's all because of you, fucking off to that mental home,' he yelled.

Frankie was behind his seat, waggling her shoulders and moving her lips to his voice.

Our mother rolled her eyes. 'For fuck's sake, Frank, will you please shut up. You've beat the granny out of them and made us all feel miserable all the way here. What more do you want?'

We opened the car doors to the sounds of 'Tie a Yellow Ribbon', blaring from a speaker hanging out of Granny Ivy's window. By the time Granddad Noah arrived, an hour or so later, we'd listened to it another thirty times, so it was with some relief that it was switched off once the old man had made his grand entrance on the arm of his eldest son.

The next hour was spent listening to his stories of the white light, and viewing his disgusting, yet very impressive scar.

Joseph offered to go and get some more alcohol and asked me to help him. I tried to say no, but my father insisted.

'Come on, Mikey,' Joseph said. 'I'm taking your Granddad's Rolls-Royce.'

I had never been allowed to go near Granddad's car before. I got in expecting to find a jacuzzi, at the very least. In fact it was nothing special inside, apart from its blue-tinted windows that meant no one could see inside.

Perfect for Joseph.

He parked the car in a cemetery and, like a giant slug, pulled himself through the gap in the front seats and into the back with me. He ordered me to strip, but before I could even remove my jumper, I was spun around against the rear window and he was tunnelling through the layers of my clothing.

In between gasping licks he asked if I liked what he was doing. I refused to say yes, but didn't dare say no. So I hummed a little and gazed outside. I counted the gravestones that surrounded the car. I could see a woman sitting on a bench. Even if I pressed my body to the window she wouldn't see me. From the outside those windows were walls.

As Joseph unbuckled, I thought of school, the mental home, and my grandfather's heart surgery; anything but Joseph, jerking behind me. As his jerks lost rhythm, he fired onto my back and I felt the shower of sticky splats as they landed across my spine.

We drove into the car park of an off licence, and Joseph casually asked me about my bruises. 'How many times does he beat you?' he said. 'Why does he? What else does he do? What can I do to help?'

I looked at his smug face. I knew he would never do anything for me. He was quite happy to get me a beating for refusing him.

As Joseph and I queued in the shop, I asked if I could wait by the car. I stood by the great blue monster and vomited, bringing up chunks of my uncle: his taste, his smell. I cried and retched and cried some more.

As Joseph appeared around the corner, I wiped my mouth clean.

'You all right?'

'Yep.'

He wouldn't have noticed. He had got what he wanted.

I held onto the bag of bottles, staring ahead as he drove.

He gave me a crooked smirk, then turned up the volume on the tape. Some Jesus loves me ditty rumbled from the speakers beneath the seats. Joseph tapped at the wheel and sang along.

Joseph didn't love me. He wouldn't help me. Why would he? He was getting exactly what he wanted. The realisation that I was trapped made me feel sick and scared.

Granddad Noah made a great recovery. His mended heart was working perfectly. He even bragged he could two-foot jump a fence.

Then Ivy died and broke it again.

That night a huge crowd gathered outside the pink trailer. Word spread fast. People from all over the country wanted to pay their respects to a great queen of the Romanies.

It was a beautiful night and no one noticed when I slipped out and ran down to the Koi pond. The stars were so bright I could see the energy burning under their skin and the full moon reflecting shards of light across the hundreds of cars and trucks that filled the entire grounds.

One of the carp had been floating around the surface of the water for four days now. Every now and again, another fish would come to the surface to take a bite out of him. He was pure white; a great ghost of a fish.

I sat beside the pond, thinking about the birthdays and Christmases we had spent in the pink caravan, eagerly opening our presents – Granny Ivy would always re-wrap and give my mother the present my mother had given her the year before. I thought about Joseph, filling the couch with his bulk, sucking on raw bacon and fingering his belly button; Frankie and I being paid to sing songs; sitting around the trailer steps, and listening to countless relatives celebrating. I remembered Aunt Prissy delicately polishing crockery as Granny Ivy, up on her stool behind her, combed her curtain of black hair.

Through the beauty of the silence around me came a great wave of a mournful song from the trailer.

Granny Ivy was dead.

A looming shape appeared in the dark. It was Joseph. I watched silently as he crashed down onto the lawn. He wailed like a wounded beast.

'Mum, oh Mum.'

To hear my giant of an uncle, crying uncontrollably, was awful. I walked over to comfort him. He climbed to his knees, pinning my arms to my sides with his the tightness of his grip.

'Please don't cry,' I said.

He leaned back onto his knees and looked into my face. I could see the brightness of his eyes, which were full of tears.

'I love you, Mikey.' His grip tightened around me. 'Please don't ever leave me.'

I stood, dumbfounded.

'Your poor granny has died.' His voice was distorted with grief.

I began to sob. As he wept I raised my arms and cradled his head. 'I won't, Uncle Joseph, on my life I won't.'

I wept for Joseph, my granny Ivy and me.

Back at the trailer Granny Ivy's giant bottle of oxygen had finally been switched off, but she was still sitting in her chair. She was even smaller than when I last saw her;

her tiny legs and pink moccasin slippers dangled a foot from the floor like those of a little girl, and a tea-towel had been tied around her head with a huge knot at the top to stop her mouth from falling open. She looked like a tiny drag queen.

How wonderful she was. How strong to have made it all this way. I remembered a picture of her taken at a theme park holding a giant ice cream. It was the length of her whole torso and she had to grasp it with both hands.

I thought of her soft childlike voice, telling stories about our history. 'We came over here from Egypt years ago! Who do you think helped build them pointy cuvas, eh?' She meant the pyramids.

Granny Ivy loved me. 'Don't you ever listen to them saying bad things about you,' she would say. 'I promise you my boy, when you get to the right age, you'll show 'em all. You're gonna break hearts, my little sweetheart.'

I knew I would miss her so much.

Two days later the mortuary returned her body through the front window of her trailer in a grand coffin that was triple her size. Every piece of furniture had been removed from the front room, and she lay in state there. The silk under the open lid of her coffin was a handcrafted mosaic of *The Last Supper*.

The cars never left, and over the next few days more arrived. We stayed in Uncle Tory's house, us children all bunched up like fleas in cousin Noah's room, while the adults never slept.

It was nearly three weeks before the lid on the coffin was closed and Granny Ivy was finally laid to rest. Her features had already begun to sink after just one. Her coffin was carried for two miles by her beloved Noah and their sons, followed by more than a hundred cars; she made the local radio that day because traffic was stopped for miles around.

14

Moving On

I was eleven when my father sold our plot at Warren Woods. It was the end of an era and a good time to go.

By that time many of the other residents had decided to move on, selling their plots for very generous prices to the Irish Travellers who had arrived in a tidal wave, fulfilling Mr Donoghue's oft-repeated prophecy that they would take over. They lived not just one family to a plot, but as many as they could fit, and within a few weeks of the arrival of the first families, our site had begun to show the scars of their invading culture: piles of rubbish, old car parts, the fences kicked down.

Our plot was sold almost immediately, giving my father the money he needed to prepare us for the road. He bought two caravans, one for him and my mother, Henry-Joe and Jimmy, and the other for Frankie and me. They came from a company that catered specifically for the needs of Gypsy people. Roma was the brand name, and they had done their research. Their trailers were monstrosities, created to mimic miniature palaces. Garish, flamboyant and overtly camp, we couldn't move for polished steel, mirrored cabinets and chrome. Every surface was carved from white, polished timber with a mirrored effect, and not one cupboard was without a glass window, so that the woman of the house could display her Crown Derby.

Gypsies are seldom poor, and since they rarely stay put, they have fewer ways to spend their cash, so they stack up on flashy jewellery and designer trailers, trade their cars in for new models every year and splash out on designer gear. The women, with little else to do but clean, often do so in full make-up, Gucci mini-dresses and Jimmy Choos. Though the regulation rubber gloves, hair in a bun and a fag hanging on the lip tarnishes the image somewhat.

My father was excited about going on the open road. My mother had no choice, the decision was his, but she seemed happy enough. The plan was that we would move from place to place, right across the country, before finding somewhere to settle for winter.

The night we finished school I sobbed myself to sleep. There were so many things I still had to learn. And I didn't want to leave Mrs Kerr.

In our final week, the class had gone to the Natural History Museum to see an exhibition about ancient Egypt. We Gypsy children were never allowed to go on school trips. Our parents didn't trust the teachers, so any permission slip would be chucked straight in the bin. This time, realising how much I wanted to go, Mrs Kerr drove to Warren Woods to ask my mother. It was a brave thing to do.

'I can't tell you just how enthusiastic your wee 'un is about this topic, Mrs Walsh. I personally would very much like to have him with me,' she said.

Mother smiled politely. 'No.'

And that was that. Mrs Kerr reluctantly gave up and left. Mother stared after her.

'Nosey old witch,' she muttered.

In truth Mrs Kerr had blown any possibility of my

mother's trust or approval a couple of months earlier, when she had sent each of us home with a permission slip for us to view a sex-education video.

Mother had been sitting in the front of the car with Granny Bettie when I passed the sordid invitation to her. 'What's this for then?' squawked old Bettie as my mother unfolded the sheet of paper.

'Sex education,' I announced enthusiastically.

In a split second and with the precision of a Ninja assassin, old Bettie gave me a karate chop to the side of the neck.

'Don't let me hear you ever say that word in front of me again, you little cunt.'

I was baffled, since I had no idea what sex was, and certainly didn't associate it with what Uncle Joseph was doing to me every week.

It was in this moment of excruciating pain that I had my first lessons in the words that should never be spoken in front of a Gypsy woman. Any sexual term was banned, as was any reference to 'women's trouble' and mention of these would earn me a chop to the neck. The exceptions were the words fuck and cunt which, despite their vulgarity, had slipped through the net of taboo words. Both men and women used them constantly. When Frankie and I asked our mother what dinner would be, she would almost always bark, 'a pig's cunt', before lapsing into a silent fit of guilt. We would pester all the time, just to get her to say it for us.

It seems ironic that most sexual terms were banned, yet most Gypsies, both men and women, used an abundance of foul language in almost every sentence, but that was the rule.

Mrs Kerr's attempt to give us sex education went down so badly that her name was mud for ever after and when it came to the Natural History Museum outing, her approach was doomed from the outset. Not only was she turned away, but I was beaten for having encouraged her to come to our home, even though I hadn't known she was coming.

A few days later Mrs Kerr drew me to one side at lunch break. She dug through her handbag, and said that she had a surprise for me – she had brought me back a blue scarab beetle charm from the exhibition.

She placed it in my palm. It was the most wonderful gift I had ever received, but I found it almost too hard to cope with such kindness.

'Thank you so much,' I whispered, trying and failing to hold back my tears.

She put her arms around me and gave me a hug. 'You are more than welcome, my pet.'

Days later, I left the school without being able to say goodbye to her. I never went to school again. I was almost eleven, and expected to go to work, like other Gypsy men.

I often wish I could see Mrs Kerr again, and thank her for what she did for me. I can never hear a Scottish accent without thinking of her.

While my parents dismantled the contents of the trailers, ready to leave, I slipped out to the stable. After Kevin's death it had fallen into disrepair and become no more than a storage place, because everyone in the camp swore it was haunted by his ghost. But I didn't mind the idea of that; I had liked Kevin and couldn't imagine his spirit ever wanting to harm me.

In place of Kevin's furniture there were bags of rubbish, my father's tools and my mother's tumble dryer. This place was both my sanctuary and my torture chamber. My father still used it as a place to beat me for wetting the bed.

Four years on it was still so bad that I hated to sleep. I would refuse to drink all evening and spend twenty minutes in the loo before going to bed. Once there I'd lie, eyes wide open, praying that it wouldn't happen again. Eventually, despite my efforts, I would fall asleep, only to wake in a wet patch. That meant a beating in the stable, then a public stripping, followed by the fire hose. But despite its association with my father's violence, I liked the stable; I knew that in there I could be alone.

My mother was the only other person who would come in during the day.

'And what are you up to?' she would say with a smile as she brought in a basket of wet clothes. I would just hold up my He-Man figures.

'Oh, are the goodies or the baddies winning today?' she would ask.

'The baddies.'

I would watch as she hummed a Patsy Cline tune while loading up the dryer.

'Well make sure you don't mess with these switches,' she would say, and hurry past with her empty basket, still singing as she left the stable. Her songs were always sad ones, and she had a voice that could reach right inside you and grab your most hidden emotions.

The old tumble dryer was my comforter and I loved it. I would lean against it, wrapping my arms around its tin bulk, feeling its rumbling warmth. Now we were going, and my private hiding place would be gone. In the caravan there would be nowhere to escape, and no friendly dryer. I wanted to store it all in my mind, before my father dismantled it the following day.

I wondered where my father would beat me, once we were on the road. Would he find some kind of tent? One thing was for sure, I would be glad to see the back of the hosepipe. And Joseph. I wouldn't have to go to that awful yard every week and be left alone with him.

I hated it, and hated him. Suddenly it dawned on me that going on the move might be the best thing ever to happen to me.

We didn't leave alone. The first to sign up to the convoy were my mother's two sisters, Nancy and Minnie, along with their families.

Aunt Minnie, queen of the shoplifting circuit, had recently given me my first ever glimpse of boob, having lobbed one of hers out and jiggled it around in front of me. She looked even more like Cruella De Vil than before, in a garish sweater that was supposed to be designer and had 'Channel' stitched in huge gold letters across the back of it, which rather gave the game away. She and her husband Jaybus now had three kids; two boys had come along after Romaine.

Aunt Nancy had been brainwashed by Granny Bettie into believing she was the 'Bardot' of the family, but she was in fact a carbon copy of her rather plain mother, only with a fatter backside and dyed blond hair cut into a crash-helmet-shaped mullet on top, with the rest so long she could sit on it. Her husband Uncle Matthew was the only

Gypsy man ever to wash dishes and together they had four small children.

Uncle Matthew also brought along his most trusted dossa, Kenny, a sorrowful-looking man with a face as flat as a witch's tit and an arch in his brow that could put Jack Nicholson to shame.

The rest of the convoy was composed of the cling-ons: two newlywed couples, with a baby each, plus the infamous Finneys – Julie-Anne, Sam and their kids. They were like the Addams Family in a trailer.

Julie-Anne was a well-known fighting woman the size of a small tractor. She'd gained the nickname Big Bad Binney for publicly beating not one, but four men who thought it wise to pick on her husband Sam at a wedding reception. Sam was around the size of one of Julie-Anne's arms, with a face like a Victorian serial killer and a mouth full of pointy black teeth. Challengers rarely bothered Sam, although we would often come home from work to find out that Binney had gained yet another notch in her belt while she'd waited for the washing to dry. Together, she and Sam had eight children: five girls, all exactly the same as Julie-Anne, and three boys all the same as Sam.

Tagging along at the last minute came my mother's youngest brother Jimmy. He had just got married to a woman almost twice his age. At thirty-five Rayleen would have been condemned to be a spinster for ever if it weren't for twenty-one-year-old Jimmy stepping in.

The day before we left, we went to Tory Manor to say goodbye to my father's family. From the moment we got there Joseph hung around me, but I made sure to stay as close as possible to the crowd, never giving him a chance to pull me away for a last goodbye fumble. Not that he didn't try. As the family chattered away he came up behind me and nudged me, rolling his eyes, winking and nodding to signal a quick getaway.

'Let's go,' he whispered.

I stared at him, then turned to Aunt Maudie. 'Those are amazing shoes, Auntie.'

'Awww, thank you!' she shrieked, lifting her foot and shaking it around. She was wearing stilettos with clear straps and thick plastic soles filled with water, rainbow glitter and with a tiny gold scale model of the Eiffel Tower welded inside each heel.

Joseph, sulking, slunk back into his trailer.

I was sad to leave our little gang of friends behind but we were sure we would soon see them all again. Their families promised to travel up and join our convoy from time to time, and we thought we'd go back and visit them.

But we never saw most of them again.

Just over a year later, our cousins Olive and Twizzel were killed in a car crash. Olive, still only thirteen, was, like so many Gypsy children that age, already driving. She was at the wheel, with Twizzel beside her, when their car was hit by a cargo lorry, killing both girls instantly. I missed them terribly.

We never saw the Donoghue girls again either, or Horace. His father died soon after we left, and he had to take over as the man of the family. Then his mother ran off with Uncle Horace's dossa. Horace was left behind to look after his elderly grandmother. The only one I was to see again was Jamie-Leigh, the Gypsy princess with her gorgeous face and gutter mouth. I loved Jamie-Leigh for her courage and confidence and I missed her humour and energy so much. I never dreamed it would be more than three years before I would see her again.

By the time we set off there were seven vans, five cars, eleven caravans, all silver plated, and two huge tipper lorries; both were sprayed in orange, yellow and black stripes and stacked to the brim with washing machines, toilet tents, awnings, dog kennels, dogs, Tarmac tools and spinning wash lines. My father was driving his lorry, towing the bigger caravan, while my mother was driving the car, towing the little one. I made sure I rode with her.

We were a convoy of dirt-eating, rough-arsed, stereotypical, Gypsy folk and we got many a horrified look from drivers on the motorway as we headed north. The plan was to move from camp to camp every few weeks, eventually making our way back down south when the winter came.

Word was the Gypsies from the north were a lot more peaceful than those in the south. I was relieved. We would be miles from the boxing club and those who revered the Walsh name. There would, I prayed, be no need to fight.

Gypsy encampments are everywhere. Most are secluded, hidden away down inconspicuous back roads. A few are slap bang in the middle of a community, but most of these don't last long, because they attract a lot of public complaints. We hoped to find camps of the more discreet kind, but by the time we went on the road the problems were mounting.

Irish Travellers hadn't just taken over Warren Woods, they seemed to be everywhere. We called them

Hedgemumpers, a Gypsy term for people who were not fussy about their living conditions. Hedgemumpers would set up camp anywhere: on the side of a motorway, or even in the centre of a local car park. This type of traveller had given us the worst public image, creating litter and chaos and taking everything that wasn't nailed to the ground. There were very few Romany Gypsies who lived this way.

We travelled north assuming we would be welcomed into established Romany camps. But we were wrong. Fearful that we were among the ever-increasing band of Irish Travellers, camp owners refused to unlock their gates. My father and the other men tried to reassure them that we were Romanies, but as soon as they heard we had come from the south, they distrusted us. By that time there were five Irish Travellers to every Romany in southern England, and they were convinced that we must have Travellers in our convoy.

Even camps we had booked in advance backed out once we arrived. On our first day, after travelling for hours, we were turned away from four different places. The people in the last camp we tried refused to even let us speak, yelling 'fuck off' as soon as they saw us.

We had no choice but to join the Hedgemumpers. We set up camp that night in an empty truck stop, just outside a large northern town. Each of the families found their spot and within a few minutes the legs were wound down on the trailers and the dogs set free from the backs of the lorries. As the women all scattered into the trees to find a decent place to relieve themselves, the men walked off to a nearby garage, taking several buckets to collect water.

I leaped onto the back of our lorry to search for our

doorstep. The sky was darkening, and the clouds were bruised with pinks and blues, curling and intertwining like lava around the setting sun. There was no electric light apart from the street lamps and no one in sight. In the distance I could see the river of twinkling lights that was the motorway and I inhaled the stench of pollution and petrol fumes.

With no one around I unzipped myself and peed onto the tarmac below the lorry.

Then Uncle Matthew's dossa appeared from nowhere, and I jumped backward in shock.

Red-faced I turned to pick up the doorstep from the lorry floor.

'You need a hand taking that off?'

'Its all right, I've got it.'

As I tilted the doorstep off the side of the lorry, he reached up, taking it from me and lowering it to the floor.

'Thank you.'

'Are you OK getting down?'

He reached up and lifted me, although I could have managed alone. 'You're definitely Frank's boy. You look just like him,' he said, smiling. 'You must be little Frankie?'

'No, that's my sister. I'm Mikey.'

He wiped his hand on his sweater and held it out to me.

'Well, I'm Kenny. I work for your uncle Matthew.'

I took his hand and he shook mine. It was the first time I had ever been greeted with a shaking of hands.

'Well, I'll see you later, Mikey. I gotta get the legs down on this trailer.'

He walked away and I stared after him.

He and I were probably the most despised two people

in the camp. Yet he had treated me politely and kindly. And in doing so he had touched the lonely, lost place inside me. Perhaps I had a friend.

Minutes later the men and women returned. The men built a campfire and the women cooked. We all sat round the fire and there were stories, songs, jokes, debates and beer after beer after beer.

After a final group toilet visit, the women retired to their trailers and it wasn't long before the men's discussion turned to the enemy: the Irish Travellers. I sat and listened as one man after another shared his fears and spoke of attacks by the Travellers on the Gypsies. The light from the fire lit their faces as they told of fighting champions who had been stabbed, shot and crippled by Travellers, attacking in huge groups.

The worst story of all came from Uncle Matthew: one of the elders had been ambushed at his daughter's wedding, tied between two vehicles and pulled apart.

After this the only sound was the crack and snap of the fire. The men's faces looked empty. The catalogue of horrific stories made them realise how serious things had become. The threat of the Irish Travellers loomed over us all.

Eventually Kenny changed the mood by pulling several lumps of coal from the fire and juggling with them. Roars of laughter erupted from the group, as one by one, they all had a turn. I covered my face and chuckled at my father's attempt. He squealed like a pig, trying to juggle a single coal, and hurled the fiery chunk into his face in a panic. It was an uplifting end to the night.

As the party began to clear Kenny took a seat next to me.

'How are you, Walsh boy?' he slurred. I could smell the alcohol on his breath.

'You're drunk.'

He nodded, taking a long drag of his cigarette. 'I wanna show you something.' He pointed up towards a cluster of stars. 'Look up there . . . Kenny's pot.'

'What?'

'That group of stars up there. You see it?'

It was the Big Dipper. But how was I to know back then? From that moment on I would always know it as 'Kenny's Pot'.

Sitting there by the dying embers of the fire Kenny told me about his wife and little girl. 'Do you wanna see a picture?'

He reached into his shirt pocket, pulling out an old wallet, and from it three passport-sized photos. He passed them over. At first I couldn't make them out. The glow from the fire was highlighting an overlay of greasy fingerprints. Eventually I made out a mugshot of someone who looked like the serial killer, Rose West.

'That's the wife . . . isn't she beautiful?'

What could I say?

'She's stunning.'

The other two were of a happier, less distressed-looking Kenny, holding on his lap a little girl. The resemblance between father and daughter was astonishing.

'Where are they now?'

He heaved a sigh, lighting up another cigarette

'I don't know. She left me over a year ago and took my baby with her.'

He raised the cigarette to his mouth and paused. Then,

he let out a silent wail. I followed my instinct and did a most uncommon thing. I put my arms around him. And he wept until my neck was drenched with tears.

Later I lay in my bunk, staring at the ceiling.

There was a rumble of thunder. A storm was coming. Lightning lit the sky, and rain began to fall; huge drops like rocks, crashing faster and faster on the tin roof in an up-tempo samba.

From behind the sliding door I could hear Frankie, muttering and swearing in her sleep. I thought about Kenny, my new friend. He didn't really know, or understand, what I was going through. I knew that.

I was a messed-up boy, and he was a dossa; both of us outcasts. But Kenny treated me like a human being, he cared what I thought and spoke about things other than fighting and money. He made me feel as if, just for a moment, I mattered, and for that I loved him.

15

Twelve-Year-Old Man

For the next few months we travelled. We managed to find a few Gypsy camps that would take us in, and we would stay for a few weeks, while my father and the other men found work.

With the dossas he'd had working for him down south no longer around, my father had only two people to put on a job: me – and him. I was almost twelve years old, and in Gypsy terms 'of age'. It was time to go out with him and learn my trade.

No Gypsy man at that time was trained in how to do any kind of construction, building or home improvement work. But regardless of a lack of training or skills, they managed to make a very successful living from these trades.

Some were much more professional than others, but it was a rarity for a Gypsy man to do a good job for anyone. Especially if money were to change hands before a job was done; in that case the customer would almost certainly get nothing at all. And in some cases, given the state of the building work I've witnessed, they'd probably have been better off.

My father's speciality was re-surfacing driveways, so this was the 'trade' I was to learn. On my first day out with him, buried beneath an extra-large boiler suit and unable even to grip a shovel correctly, I couldn't help but think I was only there because he had no other choice. He didn't want to be on a job with me any more than I wanted to be on one with him. But there was no one else, so we had to make it work somehow. Not that my father intended to do any actual work, as I soon discovered. His role was to be the foreman, do the talking, and order me around.

Our working day soon settled into a pattern. Thankfully by this time I had stopped wetting the bed, so I was spared the pain and humiliation of a public beating. Instead I would be woken at six and told to fill up the tar drums, roll them up onto the lorry and strap them down, then do a checklist of all the tools we needed for the day and make sure we had them at the ready. Once we set off, our first stop was the local quarry, where I would shovel a ton or so of pink grit onto the back of the lorry. It was around 70 per cent dust and I had to make sure it was well covered as even a slight rainstorm could ruin it. By the time we left the quarry each morning, I was painted head to toe, eyelashes to teeth, in a thick coat of hot pink paste.

After that my father would stop at a local baker to load up on custard tarts, pastries and iced buns. He was diabetic, but cheated like holy hell. His first communication with me would be a grudging offer of something from one of the bakery's paper bags. That was the closest we came to a 'Good morning, how are you?' moment. I'd eat a doughnut or an iced bun while he, breathing heavily, sucked on several sweet cakes.

After the sugar binge was over, he would be ready for the hunt. Already exhausted, I would fall asleep to the strains of his Roy Orbison/Doris Day tape mix, while my father would scan the streets for his first 'customer'. We'd thread in and out of small villages, looking for the perfect neighbourhood; one where the houses had driveways. Once he had found a likely house, my father would turn into a performance artist of extraordinary skill, with a tongue that rolled out lines as eloquently as a Shakespearian pro.

Animated, charming and gracious, the old bastard was a marvel to watch. He would greet the house-owner in such a familiar manner that it would convince them he was already an acquaintance. After several minutes of general chit-chat he would find just the right moment to hit them with the 'offer of the day'. He had been working on a nearby project, he would explain, and had overestimated how much tarmac he would need. Rather than let it go to waste, he would tarmac the customer's driveway for the ridiculously small sum of ten pounds.

Only the badly off, tight-fisted or gullible would fall for it, but there seemed to be no shortage of them around. But then my father was like a hunter; he bragged that he could smell a naive pensioner from miles away.

Taking advantage of an elderly person's lack of company, he would even fool them into believing that his 'bargain offer' was all down to the fact that his own father had done their driveway many years before. With no idea whether he was telling the truth or not, most would give him the benefit of the doubt and nod happily in agreement.

And so we would set to work. I would scrape away the weeds while my father spread the barrels of watered-down tar over the driveway. Then, filling a wheelbarrow with the pink grit, I would have to spread it onto the drive as evenly and as thinly as possible.

My father gave orders and I obeyed. Other than that,

we didn't speak. I was expected to know how to do everything; there was no room or time for mistakes. We had to get the job done and be gone as soon as we could.

Once we had finished, the driveway would look good. But we knew that as soon as it rained the grit would turn to sludge, and all that would be left was a washed-out mess. With no time to lose, the victim would be called out to inspect their wonderful new drive. Then, once they had admired it, he would hit them with the actual price, bumping up the total to ten pounds a square metre. When they protested, he would claim it had been their mistake for mishearing what he had told them in the first place.

When we returned from work I had to re-fill the tar barrels he had bought, or sometimes stolen from a motorway road works area. I would often be on the back of the lorry all evening, separating one fresh barrel of tar into three empties, then, topping up all four with the water hose to get more distance out of it.

By the end of the evening I would fall into bed, exhausted, only to go through the same thing again the next day, often seven days a week.

All of the convoy were dealing in similar lines. Some did the same as my father, others sold carpets, tiled roofs, put in windows or did any other kind of job that could be botched to look good long enough to extort cash.

Before we moved north, my father had dealt in stolen cars as a sideline. Together with one of his dossas, Wayne, who had been a professional car thief before he came to work for us, my father would drive us through a local town, looking for the right kind of cars. Souped-up vans, or anything that had baby boots, boxing gloves, horseshoes or rosaries hanging from the mirror were left alone. These things were like a kind of secret tag that let fellow Gypsies know not to steal from one of their own. My father and Wayne would look for posh cars with any hint of a bag or credit card inside. When they spotted one, Wayne would be let loose to get into the car and follow us home in it.

The next day, Wayne and my mother would pose as a rich couple, going into expensive chain stores and spending as much as they could on the credit cards stolen from the car. They would have spent the night before practising the signature on the card and getting into character. My father had them buy every household appliance and item of clothing we could possibly make a future buck on, following them around the shops and pointing out what he wanted. Wayne had burnt lips and fingers from his endless smoking, but with a major scrub up and an Armani suit, bought with an earlier stolen card, he could almost pass as a gentleman; unlike my father who looked like the Godfather in the gutter in whatever he put on. My mother's costume – a pink pencil skirt suit with colossal shoulder pads and a large-brimmed white hat – could have come straight from Krystle Carrington from her favourite show.

While the two of them spent on the stolen cards, the stolen car would be 'ringed up' – my father's term for disguising the car and selling it on.

When we moved north Wayne chose not to come, so the car trade became no more than an occasional sideline for my father, and his main business was the re-surfacing. We would work an area until work ran dry, or a customer involved the police.

A few months into our northern tour, we had settled on

a campsite and I was shovelling some well-earned beans on toast into my mouth, when a stranger marched up to our plot. He was young and stocky, with a huge gut that dangled below his vest and greasy hair that flopped about his face. He stood in the doorway of the trailer.

'You Frank's boy?'

A forkful of toast lodged in my throat and my heart began to thump as I realised what was coming. The Walsh reputation had not, after all, been left down south. This was my first challenger.

'Yep.'

Without another word he squared up; his greasy curls whipped at his forehead and his belly jiggled as he danced around and jabbed the air with his fists. 'Get up,' he hissed.

My father, Frankie and Aunt Minnie came out of the other caravan, all three with cigarettes in mouths. At thirteen, Frankie was now an 'out of the closet' smoker.

I put down my plate. 'What have I done?'

The boy didn't answer; he just kept on jiggling and beckoning me to come.

'Where have you come from, Mush?' my father asked him.

The boy paused and then bowed as if he were meeting royalty. 'Liverpool, uncle. I'm Basher Bill's boy.'

My father tilted his chin upwards in acknowledgement.

'Well at least the little bastard's polite,' muttered Aunt Minnie.

'How old are you?' Frankie asked.

'Seventeen.'

'Piss off, shitty arse, the boy's not old enough yet,' said Aunt Minnie.

But my father yanked me out of my chair. 'Put your hands up, Mikey.'

Aunt Minnie's eyes rolled. 'Frank, he's a child.'

My father didn't even look at her.

'Mikey, if you don't get up and fight that boy, I'm gonna kick you all the way to Dover.'

I took a step forward and the boy began to bounce again. Reluctantly I mirrored his stance and then rushed at him. Straight into a punch. After four or five more I was down and the fight was over. I didn't bleed. I didn't cry. I didn't even open my mouth. I got up from the concrete, brushed myself off and sat back inside, with Frankie and Aunt Minnie following closely behind.

My father gave the boy a begrudging 'congratulations', and shook his hand. Then, as the boy smiled proudly, my father drew his fist back and punched him in the teeth. The boy slammed into the side of his van and slid to the floor. He got up and clambered into it like a terrified rabbit.

'Now go and bring your fat cunt father down here,' my father yelled.

The van sped from the camp in a cloud of dust.

My father stuck his head through the open window of the trailer, wiping the dust from his eyes. 'Get out here.'

I hesitated. I knew that look. He was enraged and looking for someone to vent his fury on. He let out a grunt. 'Get. Out. Here.'

As I stood, uncertain what to do, he came charging towards the door.

'Run, Mikey,' shouted Frankie.

I leaped for the door, foolishly hoping I could outrun

him. Seconds later the toe of his boot kicked into my tail-
bone. I fell, face first, and my chin smashed against the
concrete.

He laughed. 'Go on then, cry for your old dad.'

I crawled off the plot, choking up blood, and hobbled
away.

'You're useless, no good even as a dog,' he called after
me.

I gained speed, heading towards the nearby lorry park
where Kenny's trailer was. As a mere dossa he wasn't
allowed to join us in the camp. An injury in the centre of
my face pumped blood backwards across my cheeks as the
wind hit my skin and the air whistled past my ears. The
inside of my mouth had filled with blood, but I couldn't
open my lips to spit.

I turned into the lorry park and slammed against Kenny's
trailer. I tapped at the windows, blood dribbling down from
the sides of my mouth. I banged on the door and tried the
handle. It was locked. There was no reply. Kenny was still
out at work with Uncle Matthew.

I turned around and dived between the wheels of our
lorry, where I curled into a tight ball, hoping that my father
wouldn't come to find me.

I held my breath. Held my anger. Held my tears. I trapped
it all behind my teeth, locking it behind my jaw, my neck,
my throat and my chest. I squeezed my eyes shut to stop
the tears.

I hated myself. I hated my life. I hated what I had become
– a punch bag, a dog, a slave and a lost cause. A joke, to
my father, his family and the whole Gypsy race.

I have to leave this place, I thought. I don't belong here.

But at only twelve, where could I go? This life is all that I knew. I was trapped.

With that realisation I could no longer hold back the tears. I tightened my mouth, sobbing angrily, burbling blood down my neck and my chin as I tried to catch my breath. I felt a loose piece of cartilage suck up into my nasal passage and soon my fear and anger and grief were overshadowed by the waves of pain.

I dug my fingernails into my forearms. After the initial shock had gone I realised that my nose was broken and my two front teeth had pierced through the skin beneath my bottom lip, fastening my mouth shut. I fiddled with the lumps in my mouth with my tongue, clearing away the skin tangled between the gaps in my teeth.

I heard the sounds of UB40 and heavy wheels crushing over the grit on the road. My mother was back from town with Henry-Joe and Jimmy. Minutes later I heard the scuttle of feet across the stones and high-pitched whispers between intakes of smoke.

My mother and Aunt Minnie.

They moved around the car park, calling my name softly. Then my mother spotted me. She leaned over me, tutting. 'Let's have a look.'

She lifted my head and the pain made me hiss. A lump of blood sprang out, catching her neck. She smacked it off as if it was a mosquito.

'Minnie, come here,' she said. 'Hold his chin a minute, will you?'

My mother pulled at my lips and I screamed through my teeth, which remained firmly embedded.

They each grabbed one of my arms. As I rose to my

feet, Aunt Minnie tried to brush me down. 'Oh, his lovely clothes, Bettie – look.'

'Never mind his clothes. Let's get back and get his mouth open.'

We walked back, the two women blanketing me with their bodies.

'Your father's gone to the pub with Uncle Jaybus,' my mother said. 'You've no need to worry.'

Back at the trailer, they lowered me to the ground, next to the outside tap. Then they started to manoeuvre my lips, slapping at each other's hands and arguing as if they were trying to solve a Rubik's cube.

After a few minutes of no progress, my mother stopped. 'Get me the tin out of the cupboard,' she said.

Aunt Minnie dashed off into the trailer to search for my mother's magic tin. I wasn't sure that her usual rub with a slug or piece of bloody meat would work on this. She wiped her red palms across the chest of her sweater and looked at me, pondering, while we both listened to Aunt Minnie, slamming cupboards and swearing to herself.

My mother scanned the concrete and handed me an old dustpan brush. 'Take this and squeeze on it when it's really bad, all right?'

I nodded, gripping it with both hands and trying to focus on anything other than the terrible pain. I stared into my mother's eyes, inches from my own: black and shiny as boiled tar. She focused on the wound, frowning and then with one, big yank, she freed my teeth.

Aunt Minnie arrived with the tin and as my mother began to rummage through it, Aunt Minnie pulled a cigarette box from her cleavage, took out a cigarette and lit it.

She took several drags and then tossed it away, before crouching down to make some butterfly stitches from band-aid and tape as my mother dabbed at the wound with antiseptic and cotton wool.

It took several weeks for my face to heal, but if I hoped that first challenge would be a one-off, or that my father might give up on making me fight, then I was soon to discover I was sadly mistaken.

We kept on moving locations, and everywhere we went there were challengers. Boys my age were seldom interested in being friends. Every camp seemed to have at least one group of over-confident young bucks with a point to prove and I would have to fight whoever came to my door.

I never won. This infuriated my father, who would take it upon himself, after every losing match, to kick me while I was down, and then head off to take on my challengers, their fathers and anyone else who cared to join in.

Soon I was living in dread of confrontation, with challengers, or with my father. Once we were back from work, I tried to stay out of his way. And every evening, when Uncle Matthew came back to his trailer from the lorry park, I would head off to the one place I felt welcome: Kenny's trailer.

16

Take Me With You

If you really want to infuriate a Gypsy man, and land yourself in a major fight, call him gay. The term is often used as an insult in the non-Gypsy world, but to Gypsy men, who pride themselves on being red-blooded males, there can be no bigger put-down.

I got used to my father calling me a poof as a sign of his contempt. He laughed, spat and screamed a dictionary of 'homo' terms at me a hundred times a day. And before I had turned ten years old, Frankie had begun doing it too. To hear her laugh as she spoke those words drove a stake into my heart and a rift between us.

The rift had first started during an argument over a can of Coke. Not content with calling me a poof, she had laughed and called me Joseph. It wasn't because Joseph was gay; no one knew that he was. Frankie called me Joseph because he was a big, fat, ugly, moody, morbid, unmarried man who ate raw meat and to be like him would be any boy's worst nightmare. What she didn't know was that she was comparing me to the man who had caused me so much suffering. Incensed, I had stabbed her in the hand with a pencil and after that she called me Joseph whenever she wanted to get at me.

I can't remember when I first realised that I really was gay. In some ways the knowledge had always been there, deep inside me. But of course I tried to deny it to myself, desperate not to be the one thing that would totally destroy me as a Gypsy. But as I approached puberty, I couldn't pretend to myself any more. It wasn't anything to do with what my uncle had done to me, but knowing that he too was attracted to the same sex left me feeling even more cursed. I lived every day, hating myself for being a freak among Gypsies. I knew I must never, ever let my family know. Although my father called me a poof every day, if he thought it was true, rather than just the worst insult he could think of, he would go ballistic and would, almost certainly, kill me.

So I kept it to myself, hating myself, hating what I was, trapped by it and terrified of somehow being found out.

By the time I was twelve I was battered by the nightmare of puberty. Body hair sprouted, my wisdom teeth appeared, and for several months my voice persistently changed mid-sentence, plunging an octave, from Kate Bush sound-alike to Barry White. Kenny found it very amusing, teasing me at every available moment. But I gave as good as I got, reminding him that he was a rather haggard twenty-six.

As the year wore on and we travelled from one site to another, most of the time I rode in Kenny's truck with him. It was a relief for me to be out of my father's sight and with someone who seemed to genuinely like me. We laughed and bantered, and he played me his collection of country music tapes, and in my sad and lonely young heart I fell in love with him. I convinced myself that he might love me too and often imagined us running away together. But of course, I didn't dare speak of this to Kenny.

Once I had turned twelve my father began teaching me

to drive, so that I could be the chauffeur for him and the other men every pub night. I got plenty of practice, since pub night was every night, but I was happy to do it because that way I got to spend the evenings with the older men and, more importantly, with Kenny. It was far better than staying at home where I had become a sitting duck for other Gypsy boys to come and beat the shit out of me. With no men around there was no one to stop them, once I was out cold. At least if I was challenged in the pub, my father and the other men would be there to see a fair fight, and to stop it if need be.

The men often managed to find a 'Gypsy friendly' pub that would provide an after-hours lock-in. I would be kept waiting, sitting quietly alongside them, chewing on the straw of a pint of orange squash till two or three in the morning.

One Friday night my father ordered that I stayed at the camp to fill the tar barrels and load them onto the back of the lorry. It was midnight before I finally crashed into bed, only to wake at two to hear my father's truck rumble onto the campsite and the sound of ten drunken men wailing out one of their favourite Elvis ballads. Frankie, on the opposite bunk, muttered 'Oh, for fuck's sake' and buried her head beneath her pillow.

The truck rumbled like a tank across the gravel, before coming to a halt in front of our trailer, its headlights left on full beam. The men poured out, and for the next half hour they took turns lurching in front of the truck to claim the spotlight and slur a drunken song. I sat up and watched them through a crack in the blind. I chuckled to myself as Kenny stumbled in front of the headlamps for his turn.

He always sang the same old Jim Reeves song, an ode

to his lost wife. 'Put your sweet lips, a little closer to the phone, let's pretend, we're together, all alone.' He sang it both word- and pitch-perfect and his voice cracking as he struggled through the final bars.

Finally the men said their goodnights, and one by one they vanished into the darkness.

Only Kenny, my father and Uncle Matthew were left.

'Goodnight then all,' said my father, stumbling towards his trailer. He struggled pathetically with the zip of the awning and once inside I could see him falling about in desperation, trying to find the door handle of the trailer. After a couple of minutes he gave up.

'Bettie!'

No answer. He pounded at the door like Fred Flintstone.

'*Bettie!*'

Suddenly there was a loud splash and the crash of smashing crockery. He had tripped and fallen into Henry-Joe and Jimmy's old bathwater, taking half a table of crockery with him.

'*Open the fffukinnn dooare!*'

The door was flung open and he finally disappeared from sight.

Now only Kenny was left outside. I slipped on some shoes and went out.

The night was humid and sticky and the smell of cigarettes and alcohol hung in the air. I opened the car door, reaching inside to turn off the beams, which were still on. For weeks I had been longing to tell Kenny how I felt. Now it seemed my opportunity had come. The walls of my stomach felt as though they were being torn apart. I needed to tell him how wonderful he was, how I would never leave him, hurt him or break his heart. I would plead with him to save me, and take me away from my father. But would he listen? Would he feel the same way? Or would he be shocked, and tell my father.

Either way, I had to take the risk.

He was leaning against the side of the truck, vomiting.

'You all right?' I asked.

'Mikey Boy!'

He wobbled upright, putting his arm around my shoulders.

Just then, a loud crash came from Uncle Matthew and Aunt Nancy's trailer, followed by screams and the chorus of their newly woken children joining in.

Uncle Matthew was known as a henpecked man, but when he got drunk he was transformed into a raving madman. His reputation, post ten pints, for being a foul-mouthed, wife-beating, destructive Mr Hyde was a colossal joke amongst the men.

But Aunt Nancy wasn't averse to throwing the odd punch herself. Living next to them was never dull. Not a week would go by without at least one trailer-rocking fight between the two of them, followed by the smashing of anything in the trailer that could make a sound. The fights usually finished with the both of them bursting out the trailer door, rolling about on the plot, and clawing at each other until a big enough group of us could tear the two of them apart.

The two of us watched from a safe distance as Matthew fell from the trailer, quickly followed by flying plates, cups and a Nintendo, which bounced off of his cowering shoulders.

'I'm going over,' said Kenny, obviously worried that his boss was about to be murdered by his wife.

I grabbed him by the arm. 'Don't, Kenny, leave them to it.'

'I gotta see if he's all right. *I'm coming, Matt,*' he bellowed, lurching towards their caravan.

My mother opened the window behind me and leaned out, her pale skin gleaming in the moonlight. 'What are you doing out here?'

'I was helping Kenny, Mum, but he's gone to Uncle Matthew's.'

My mother paused and stared at me. Then she turned inside. 'Frank, get up. Kenny's going to get himself killed.' She turned back to me. 'Mikey, go to bed before he gets out of this trailer and finds you.'

I leaped back to the trailer and into my bed. I watched through the blinds as Uncle Matthew dragged Kenny onto the plot and kicked him repeatedly in the ribs. 'You fucking (kick) Gorgia-bred (kick) bastard!'

Kenny rolled across the concrete, pleading for mercy. 'You're my friend, Matt, I love you mate, please!'

My father stepped out in his jeans and braces.

'Frank! Help me! Please!' Kenny called.

But my father watched in silence, smoke from his cigarette curling around his pitiless face, as Matthew continued to punish Kenny for interfering. Kenny was weeping uncontrollably and screaming for help. It was terrible to see him.

Eventually Matthew stopped. 'Get up, go home, pack up your stuff and get out of my sight.'

Kenny squirmed on the ground holding his guts. 'You're all I got, Matt. Please don't make me go away.'

Matthew grabbed him by the shoulders and threw him

from the plot. Kenny turned back to Matthew, holding out
his arms. Matthew picked up a rock and threw it at him.
It bounced off his brow and knocked him to the ground.

'Fuck off!'

My father walked over and passed Matthew a cigarette.
They muttered quietly, watching Kenny disappear, sobbing,
into the night.

I felt sick with grief. I watched from the window, crying
and praying that he would return and take me with him.
I grabbed my coat and boots. I had to find him before he
left without me.

The other men from the camp arrived outside, wanting
to know what had happened. As questions flew and he
started to sober up, Mr Hyde exorcised himself from
Matthew's body and he began to weep with guilt for what
he had done. He set off to Kenny's caravan at a run, calling
over his shoulder, 'I got to get him back, Frank.'

My father and the others dived into the truck once again,
charging off into the darkness, to search the roads and
fields for the missing dossa.

I crept out of the plot and into the dark.

The first place to look was the most obvious. Kenny's
small trailer was parked in the gas bottle storage yard, a
mile down the lane from the rest of us. When I got there
the main gates were locked, so I ran to the sturdiest part
of the fence, clambered over and fell face first into a burnt
orange sea of empty canisters glistening in the darkness.

Across the yard was Kenny's trailer. A faint light came
from inside and I could see a shadow, moving. I began to
battle through the army of bottles, heaving them out of
my way until I got clear and ran towards Kenny's door.

At that moment he appeared in the doorway. His face was frozen, like a man possessed. He shoved past me, picking up two new gas bottles and taking them inside with him.

'What are you doing?' I said desperately.

'Go away.'

He shoved past me again, and collected another two bottles. He carried them in, shutting the door and locking it behind him. A fearful hiss screamed from inside and in that moment I understood.

He was going to kill himself.

I leaped at the locked door, tearing it from its rusty hinges and stood, gasping for breath, in the doorway. Kenny was sobbing, matches in his hand and all four gas bottles on full blast.

'*Get out!*' he wailed, throwing a chair at me.

'*I won't,*' I shouted, taking hold of the chair and sitting on it.

He leaped at me, grabbed me by the hair and threw me from the doorway. In desperation, I climbed to my feet, leaping back inside.

The air had become thick and poisonous with gas and his face changed shapes through the distorted atmosphere. This time I made sure he couldn't get rid of me; I wrapped myself around the central leg of his table.

He threw the matches to the floor. 'Mikey, I don't want to hurt you, get out.'

I tightened my grip as he grabbed at my legs. 'No,' I screamed.

He pulled me from the table, and started dragging me across the floor. I grabbed at the base of a cupboard and he stamped on my hand. I screamed out in pain, and rushed back to the table, this time hanging on to it with my whole strength.

'Mikey,' he cried. 'Get out. Please.'

He leaned down to pick up the matches.

'I'll do it with you in here, *I swear to fucking god I will*!'

As he took several matches from the box, I clamped my eyes shut, tensing my whole body in fear.

'Kenny, please! I love you! I fucking love you! I can't live without you. You're the only thing that has ever made me feel happy in my entire life. I can't let you die and leave me here. Please, Kenny, if you have to do this, I need to go with you. I love you.'

Twenty seconds later I opened my eyes. The gas was still screaming wildly, and Kenny had slumped to the floor in a heap, weeping uncontrollably.

I leaped up and started to shut the taps on the gas bottles, struggling because two of the fingers on my right hand, where Kenny had stamped on them, were immoveable.

I grabbed each gas bottle one by one, dragging them to the trailer door, and rolling them to the ground. Once they were out, I pushed the windows wide open to rid the trailer of the overbearing stench of the gas.

Kenny didn't look at me. He pulled himself up onto his bunk and buried his face in his hands, weeping and swearing and shaking his head.

I heard my father's truck rumble into the yard. The men had returned from the hunt for Kenny and had come to check if he was here. As Uncle Matthew unlocked the gates, I rushed through the trailer, closing the windows with my left hand.

Kenny looked up. 'Mikey?'

'Yes?'

'Don't tell Matt, will you?'

The moment had passed. He was not going to say any of the things I longed to hear. I sighed.

'Of course I won't.'

The voices and the crunch of gravel approached the trailer. Uncle Matthew stepped in, with tears in his eyes.

'Kenny, I'm so sorry mate, you know what I'm like when I . . .'

'It's all right, come here.'

Kenny rose from his bunk and gripped Matthew in a masculine hug.

My father appeared in the doorway. 'I thought I told you to get the fuck to bed?'

'He's all right, Frank,' said Kenny. 'He just helped me get back to the trailer, that's all.'

My father looked me up and down, narrowing his eyes. 'What's up with your hand?'

'I trapped it between two of the tar barrels earlier on. Think I've broken my fingers.'

He shook his head. 'Got no more sense than a cat's got cunt, you ain't. Get out of the trailer, big man, and go up to bed.'

As I made my way through the yard, I could hear laughter and through the broken door of Kenny's caravan I could see the group emptying his beer fridge and settling down for part two of their drunken night. It was as if nothing had happened at all.

I walked home, my fingers throbbing, and my heart cracked. It wasn't my love that had stopped Kenny from killing us both, it was the realisation that there was someone even more pitiful and wretched than he was.

And now, after the ordeal, we were both left with a secret to bear.

When I got back I went into my parents' trailer and pulled a bottle of vodka and a box of painkilling pills from the chest, and then crept with them to my bed.

The next day I woke up with a swollen hand, a throbbing headache and a half-full bottle of vodka lying next to me.

Frankie's bunk was made and the curtains were open. I pulled back the sheets to find a blanket of vomit. I brushed the crust from my mouth, my chest, my legs and my arms, removed all my clothes, pulled on some tracksuit bottoms, then bundled up the sheets and took them out to the shed. As I waited for the washing machine to begin I glanced through the open shed door. My father's truck was gone.

I walked over into my parents' trailer. It was clean, polished, vacuumed and empty. I grabbed a bacon sandwich that had been left under a plastic cover, and took a bite. The bread was wet with cold fat, mixed with a lashing of tomato ketchup. It tasted good. Then I remembered. The family had all gone down to Tory Manor for the day. I had said I would rather stay at home.

I thought of Kenny. He hadn't said anything to my father, otherwise I would have known by now. But he didn't love me. I was just another Gypsy kid. I wasn't going anywhere, not with Kenny anyway. And I couldn't go alone – I wouldn't be able to survive in a world I didn't know.

I searched through the boys' video collection and pushed *The Wizard of Oz* into the video player. I took another bite of the sandwich, poured myself a glass of cherryade and lit up one of my father's cigarettes.

17

Regret

A few days later we were on the move again. By the time we left I still hadn't faced Kenny, so I didn't know whether he would want me to ride with him, as usual. As the convoy prepared to leave, I edged closer to his car. I watched as he double-checked the tow-bar between his car and caravan, climbing on top of it and bouncing up and down.

As he leaped to the ground, he gave me a quick look and smiled. I was so happy – perhaps we were going to be friends again, our secrets – his suicide attempt, my declaration of love – forgotten. But the next moment he slipped into his car and was gone, following the rest of the convoy out of the campsite gate.

As I stood staring after him, Aunt Minnie pulled up next to me in Old Bessie, as she liked to call her worse-for-wear Ford Sierra. After a failed attempt to get the window to wind down, she shouted, 'Get your skinny arse in here.'

Romaine was in the front seat. Aunt Minnie prodded her hard in the neck.

'Get in the back with old Minge.'

Romaine climbed over to join Frankie and baby Jimmy in the back. I slipped around the front of the bonnet and yanked open the door, to be enveloped in a cloud of smoke and cheap perfume.

'Welcome to the cool car,' Frankie hooted, swigging on

a gallon bottle of cola, before lighting up a fag. I climbed in and heaved the door shut.

The next three hours was a marathon of Aunt Minnie's Whitney, Abba and Barry White tape, mixed with bickering from the back, boy talk and terrible sing-alongs.

In the middle of a raucous version of Abba's 'Voulez-Vous', Aunt Minnie shocked me by stopping to say, 'It ain't right, Uncle Matthew's dossa wanting to spend so much time with you.'

My face flushed.

Aunt Minnie squinted over at me and carried on. 'I think he fancies you, but don't mention that, will you? Just be aware of it and stay away from him.'

I nodded.

We stopped at the motorway services where Aunt Minnie, still a hardened kleptomaniac, nipped into the shop and reappeared with wine gums and pasties.

'They were the closest things to the door,' she explained.

Our next campsite was in a dirty little town, through a dirty little road and up behind a dirty old petrol station, where we were surrounded by several overgrown fields filled with rubbish.

As we gasped with horror, Romaine giggled, 'Somebody could do with a goat.'

The battered gates to the camp hung behind an old shop. The owner, grateful to have anyone use his site, let us in without a single question. He showed us round the site, clutching an iron rake with one hand and clamping a beekeeper's hat to his head with the other, only removing it to grab the convoy's first rent payment.

The camp had only one electric box with six sockets,

and the toilet cubicle consisted of four walls and no toilet; just a large cesspool to dump toilet buckets in.

It was, without doubt, the worst camp we had ever visited. We all imagined we would move on as fast as possible. But on the first day the men found there was plenty of work, so they decided we should stay for a while.

The trailer Frankie and I lived in was parked next to the far grander one occupied by our parents and the boys. Ours had been bought third- or fourth-hand and was intended to be run into the ground, and within a month of it being left in Frankie's hands, it was well on its way.

The outer shell had a 'once white' scaly, lumpy surface, with a thick belt of oak brown that ran through the middle of it. The windows were blacked out, which was a godsend, given the disgusting orange and brown decor inside.

In the tiny kitchen area we had a non-working oven, used as storage, a non-working fridge stacked with non-perishable goodies and a microwave. Frankie's bed was made up from two broken, brown bunks, surrounded by shelf upon shelf of fancy perfume bottles she had collected. Among the fancy scents were several used moisturiser tubs, filled with old fag ends.

The other end of the trailer, next to a shower cubicle also used as storage, was my room which consisted of two narrow cupboards, a pull-out bed, and a sliding door made of petrified paper with a wood pattern stained onto it.

Frankie was not a traditional Gypsy girl. She never cleaned, never cooked and despite the Gypsy belief that girls shouldn't wash their hair while menstruating, she would never refrain from scrubbing the lacquer build-up out of her Chaka Khan do, whatever the time of the month.

She would remain asleep for most of the day, rolling over and growling 'fuck off' whenever our mother tapped on the window. But as Frankie was never willing to do any kind of housewifely chore at all, my mother was a teacher without a pupil. Around three o'clock Frankie would get up, and after an hour or so of trowelling on her make-up, she would be ready to face the world.

To get round the problem of cleaning, she would kidnap Henry-Joe and Jimmy nightly, dragging them over to our trailer so that she could 'play' with them. Once inside our trailer she would dress them in her clothes and make-up for the nightly 'game' of 'Queen Ant'. Frankie was, of course, the queen ant in question, and the boys were her willing worker ants. They would drag the queen, crippled from over-eating and unable to move (which wasn't far from the truth in Frankie's case), from one end of the trailer to the other, cleaning and tidying as they went. Frankie would lay comatose as they passed by the fridge, picking up packets of biscuits and crisps to feed her. Once they had half-killed themselves getting her onto the bed, they would leave her stuffing her face in front of a video, while they finished cleaning the trailer.

Frankie, through sheer boredom, had doubled in size since we started travelling, and was not remotely interested in shedding weight. The more my father brought up her being fat, the more she would take sick pleasure in corrupting our brothers. Especially his champion, Jimmy, who was five years old, and already running a self-made training circuit and weightlifting daily with bean cans in pillowslips. Our father had no idea that during pub hours, little Jimmy was kitted out in miniskirts, high heels and fake Chanel clip-on earrings, spoon-feeding his 'queen' a microwave toad in the hole.

Henry-Joe, now age seven, was a mass of ginger hair, with a pinched, white face. He spent most of his time teaching Jimmy ridiculous words that made no sense whatsoever. He did it so often that the words became part of his own vocabulary, and all too often both boys were considered simpletons, running around in circles, screaming gobbledygook words at the top of their lungs.

I laughed long and hard at Frankie's Queen Ant routine. My own games with the boys were more likely to be Sega ones – I spent hours with them, helping them work out the moves. I loved them dearly and enjoyed being around them, as long as my father was out of the way.

Eventually, to everyone's relief, it was decided that we should move on, to a camp in Newark. It was, apparently, a great place to be, with plenty of work and a good camp. Aunt Rayleen, wife of my mother's little brother Jimmy, told us her family had been there for weeks and had no plans to move.

'It's paradise,' she told us excitedly. 'Acres of land, hot and cold water, a nice shower block and plenty of electricity.' We liked the sound of it – hot food, clean clothes, TV and, best of all, no need for a weekly trip to the local sports centre for a decent wash.

Rayleen's three brothers were already there, and she talked about them constantly to Frankie.

'Honest to God, Frankie, you've never seen three

better-looking boys in all your life!' she repeated over and over again like a rather manic parrot.

By the time we hit the road we all knew that the oldest, Danny, was a flame-haired, muscular twenty-five-year-old stud that was divorced (his wife's fault, of course). Then there was Jay, who, according to Rayleen, looked like a young Marlon Brando, and every travelling girl in the country wanted a piece of him. And finally there was Alex, only sixteen, and already a renowned ladies' man, due to his silver tongue and fancy pick-up lines.

I could see that Uncle Jimmy's squeeze was intent on setting my sister up with one of her brothers. But what Frankie thought about it, I didn't know. She was now fourteen, which was the courting age, and meant that she was officially ripe to start dating and find a husband.

All Gypsy girls are expected to marry between the ages of sixteen and eighteen, with a limit of no more than four boyfriends to sample beforehand. More and a girl is at risk of being called a slut. And boyfriends mustn't be allowed to do more than show an interest. Gypsy men, while happy to pick up Gorgia women for sex away from the camp, want to marry a girl who has never even been kissed by another man.

The girls get the raw end of the stick. They spend their days training to become the perfect housewife, and in the meantime there is absolutely no sex before marriage, and they must not even speak of it.

The courting rules dictate that a girl also has to be officially asked out before even sharing a kiss with the boy she desires. On top of this, it is considered desperate and bad form to say yes to a date right away. The boy is expected to return with the same question at least a couple of times before getting the answer he longs for. Sadly, things often go wrong and the boys move on after a first rejection, leaving the girl heartbroken. And she can do nothing to resolve the situation. Having done the right thing and said no, for the sake of her reputation, she can only silently hope that he will come back and ask her one more time, at which point she will be allowed to say yes.

Many Gypsy girls go on to regret losing the one boy they really wanted, all because tradition dictates that they must say no when they long to say yes. And if they haven't found a husband by the age of eighteen, they risk growing old alone, condemned to be unwed spinsters by a crazy set of customs.

Girls are also not supposed to talk to men when they have their periods. We boys, hearing about this via underground means (any talk of periods was another taboo), would watch the girls like hawks, waiting to see how far a 'traditional' girl would go in avoiding us, to keep to the custom.

Frankie ignored it, just as she ignored the no hair-washing-during-your-period rule. But she was still a Gypsy girl and, like her friends, wanted to find a husband. So it was with a little more effort over her clothes and hair than usual that she prepared for the move to Newark.

I was interested in meeting Rayleen's brothers too, mainly because it was rumoured that they didn't like Uncle Tory and his sons. When I heard that, my heart soared. Finally, a group of people who weren't desperate to live in the Walsh shadow. I hoped to make friends with these boys, if only to annoy my father.

* * *

A couple of days before the move, a flurry of cleaning began. All the women, except Frankie, began scrubbing their caravans in order to make a good impression when we arrived. I was sitting in our caravan with Frankie, my mother, Aunt Rayleen and Aunt Minnie, who had come in for a coffee break, when my father arrived outside.

'Stop sitting with the women and clean the fucking van!' he bellowed.

My mother rolled her eyes. 'He's at it again is he? There's some cleaning stuff under the sink in the big trailer, Mikey.'

Five men were sitting in my parents' trailer, talking about fighting, money and the move to Newark. Most of them I knew, but one was new. His front teeth looked as if they had been filed into jagged points.

'He your oldest, Frank?' he asked.

Uncle Matthew looked up from his can of cider. 'He's the oldest boy . . . looks like him don't he?'

I kneeled down to the cupboard to find the cleaning stuff.

The snaggletooth man hissed with laughter. 'Naah, he's like his mother he is.'

I buried my head deeper into the cupboard to hide my blushing and smiled in quiet relief. I was happy to look like my mother, and grateful for someone who didn't compare me to Uncle Joseph.

'He hasn't got his mother's hair though,' laughed Uncle Jaybus. He opened the window and leaned out. 'She's the Ginger Ninja she is!'

The men laughed. I stood and looked out toward Frankie's trailer. Aunt Minnie leaned out, sticking up her two fingers. 'Shut your mouth, swell head!'

Uncle Jaybus sniggered in his goofy way, then bellowed back to his wife. 'I loves you, my ugly!'

Aunt Minnie cackled like a witch before collapsing in a coughing fit.

I ducked back down to the cupboard and picked up several dust rags, a can of polish and a dustpan and brush. I laughed, listening to the wails from the women in the other trailer.

My father walked over, pulling me up from the floor. 'How long does it take to get a few cleaning things.' He grabbed me by the shirt collar and kicked me out of the door, sending me hurtling from the top step and scattering the cleaning things.

The men laughed.

'Gotta train 'em up, see?'

The laughter erupted again.

'And don't dare walk away from it till it's spotless,' my father called after me.

My father had swapped our car for an old blue transit van, which was better able to pull the second trailer. It was caked in a light grey and brown crust from a rabbit-hunting trip the night before. A couple of the local men had grey-hounds and often went out rabbit hunting with them in the small hours, taking anyone who fancied tagging along with them. My father was not a fan of rabbit hunting, or of greyhound dogs, but it was a social sport and he went for the company.

I dusted myself off, picked up the cleaning things and went over to the van. I put a tape of fifties hits into the stereo, 'Secret Love' by Doris Day, blasted out at full volume, and right on chorus.

The men stuck their heads out of the trailer window, laughing. 'Sing along then,' shouted my father.

I smiled at my tormentors and turned it down. But I wasn't going to turn it off.

I scoured the muddy footprints from the dashboard and pulled out the rubber mats from the floor, throwing them into a bucket of water, mixed with vinegar and washing-up liquid. Then I polished the dashboard, vacuumed the floor, cleaned the windows, emptied the glove box, swept out the back (where I sneaked a quick ciggie from the packet I'd found in the glove box), hosed the outside, dried it, polished it and, finally, put it all together again.

Five encores of Doris later, I was done. I stood, rags and bucket in hand, feeling proud. Not since the old bastard brought the thing home had it looked so sharp. No longer was it a filthy work van and pub taxi, but it was now a fabulous show vehicle. My refection shone off the side of the cab.

I emptied the bucket and rinsed it out at the tap.

Uncle Jaybus leaned out. 'Good job.'

I beamed with pride. 'Thank you.'

My hands were wrinkled, and white. I rolled my wet sleeves up and took the remainder of the cleaning stuff back into the trailer.

My father leaned over Uncle Jaybus's shoulder. 'Do it again.'

'What?'

'You've put that fucking car polish all over the cab. Wash it off, and do it again.'

'You haven't even looked properly.'

He leaped from the bunk and pushed me backward,

out of the door and down the steps onto the ground. He threw out the bucket and rags after me and shouted, 'Don't answer me back, poofy boy. If I say do it again, you fucking do it.'

I climbed to my feet and picked up the bucket and the scattered rags and polish cans and stood, rooted to the spot.

Frankie appeared in the door of our trailer. 'Let the fat cunt do it himself, Mikey. Come in here now.'

My mother and Aunt Minnie leaned from the window. 'Just bring the stuff in here and come and sit down – it looks lovely, don't it, Min?'

'Yeah, Mikey, it looks lovely, come in here and have some tea.'

Heart pounding, I put down the bucket, walked up to my father's trailer and opened the door.

The group of men, who had been guffawing with laughter, fell silent.

My father's eyes darkened. 'What do you want?'

My mouth was dry. 'I want you to go and check the van.'

He rose from the bunk. 'Yeah?'

'Yes.'

He seemed to swell in size, and all I could see was his luminous yellow glare. 'You a big man now poofy boy?'

My body tensed. A swelling from the pit of my stomach rose and lodged in my neck.

'Get out and clean that motor.'

My fists clenched so tight my nails dug into my palms.

Then he hit me. A punch, deep into my ribcage. I fell backward and clutched the steel frame of the doorway either side of me.

He laughed and stepped closer.

I thought of what he had done to me over the years and how I had suffered every hour of every day, trying to make him happy. I thought of the countless times he had relished humiliating me in front of his friends and family.

He kicked his foot out towards my stomach. But as he did, I launched myself forward, tightening my fist like a rock and bringing it down, heavy and hard on the bridge of his nose.

The cartilage squeaked beneath my bare knuckles, as he kicked me out through the door. The men in the trailer dived out of the way as he crashed into my mother's Royal Dalton display. My mother, Frankie and Aunt Minnie screamed as I rolled onto the concrete for the third time that day. My father exploded from the trailer and charged at me like an enraged bull.

'Leave him alone.' My mother leaped from Frankie's doorway and onto my father's back, clawing, screaming and tearing at his face. But he grabbed her by the neck, punching her in the face before dropping her to the floor.

Frankie and Aunt Minnie, screaming and wailing, rushed over, picked her up and pulled her inside my parents' trailer.

The group of men came quietly out of the big trailer and dispersed.

My father's voice roared out. '*I'm going to kill you!*'

Laughing, crying and spitting out dirt, I climbed to my feet. '*Come on, then!*'

He swooped down on me and his fists crashed into my face, my ribs, my arms, my stomach.

Shaking with a rage I had never felt before, I screamed, spat, snarled and lashed out at him, numb to his punches, and laughing in his face. Then he lifted me over his shoulder and into Frankie's trailer.

Kettles, perfume bottles, empty chicken buckets and ashtrays were sent crashing as he threw me across the bunk and began to punch me in the head, face and eyes.

'*I hate you!*' I screamed. '*For as long as I've lived I've hated you!*'

He shouted at me to shut up, slamming me with more punches as I screamed and laughed and spat clumps of bloody snot into his face. As his energy drained, so did mine. Our chests and stomachs heaved as we stared at one another, panting and sweating. As blood began to blur my vision, without the strength left to speak, I mouthed the words, 'I hate you, Dad.'

He walked out of the trailer and I fell into blackness.

Our move was postponed because he disappeared. He didn't come back to the camp again for four days.

During those days the rain fell steadily and my body ached constantly. My wounds were healing badly and I lay, curled in my bunk, waiting for my father to return.

I knew it was not my fighting back that had made him go, but the words I had screamed at him.

'I hate you, Dad.'

Whatever hope there might have been for us, whatever tenuous bond we had hung onto, was gone. I hated him, and now he knew it. The huge love I'd felt for him as a small boy had been battered and taunted out of me, and we were both the losers. No doubt he was in some pub, hunched over a beer, bemoaning the fates that sent him me for a son.

As for me, I knew I needed to escape. It was my only

hope. Otherwise he would kill me, or I would die anyway, of the pain and shame and hurt of being everything he didn't want me to be, and nothing he did.

Eventually he returned, without a word to anyone about where he'd been. And in the days after that he only ever spoke to me to issue orders or threats.

Before we left for Newark Uncle Matthew and Aunt Nancy announced that they had decided to leave the convoy and head back south, taking Kenny with them. I was desolate.

Kenny and I hadn't spoken since 'that night'. Whenever he saw me coming towards his trailer he literally leaped out of it and ran away. But in my heart I had hoped that, in time, we could be friends again. I missed him so much – there had been no one else, ever, that I could laugh and talk and feel easy with in the way I did with him.

They left ahead of us, and everyone was upset. Losing some of our group after all those months together was hard. My mother and Aunt Minnie spent the morning hugging and crying with Aunt Nancy as the men helped Uncle Matthew and Kenny pack everything away.

With their trailers hooked on, the family sounded their car horns to signal goodbye. As the vehicles started to move, there were calls of goodbye and tears. Kenny's car was at the back, and I waved my arms and shouted 'Goodbye, Kenny,' hoping he might wave or smile, to signal peace between us.

He didn't even turn around. My aunt Minnie did though, raising a curious eyebrow at my enthusiasm, before looking back at the departing vehicles.

I didn't care. I turned and ran, through the gap in the

hedge and across the field to get to the fence at the end of the road for one last glimpse. Water sprayed up from the field, soaking me, and the long grass tangled around my feet, winding its tentacles around my shins. I ripped myself free of the grass and leaped to the fence, just in time to catch Kenny's car as it rattled by.

I waved again and saw him notice me. He turned to unwind his window and I felt wildly happy. He was going to say something, after all.

He drove by, without even looking at me. My only friend.

My world tumbled and crashed and burned.

The following night I sat in the back of the transit van as we set off for Newark. Through the tin wall separating us I could hear my mother's favourite tape begin. Barbra Streisand, singing 'Memories'.

The floor beneath me rumbled and I wrapped myself up in a quilt to lock in what I could of my body heat. The van stank of tar. I leaned close to the rumbling tin wall, now warming from the heaters in the front and I felt, as I used to in the stable, in the company of a friend. I had asked to ride in the back, preferring to be alone among the luggage, where I felt safe from my father's tongue and fist.

We travelled at dead of night, so there was nothing to see. I lay, curled on the floor, and wondered what the future held for me. My father was a pureblood, a great man, a champion bare-knuckle fighter, a Black Knight of raging firepower.

And me? I was no knight. My growing fear and mistrust of people was trapping me in a lonely inner world. I lived in fear of angering my father with my 'effeminate' traits.

I frequently locked myself into confined spaces to find sanctuary and be myself without a disapproving world ripping me to shreds. Despite my efforts, I had become everything Gypsies despise. I was gay. I had caught a disease that could only be found in the world outside, and everyone could see it. They knew. And that's why I was a slave to my father.

I lit a stolen cigarette and sat in the darkness. My whole body chanted the same thing over and over; run, run, run. Go far away and never come back.

But I was still not quite thirteen years old and couldn't imagine ever being away from my culture and my people. So I clung, with quiet desperation, to the alternative. Newark could be my chance for a new start. No one there would know about me. Our new home could mark my new life, where I would finally pummel the feelings that made me this way. I would work harder, and make my father proud of his heir. I had to. Despite the crushing rules, I was proud of being a Gypsy. It was who I was.

Somehow, this time, I would make it work.

18

A New Start

As the van's brakes slammed on and we lurched over a ramp in the road, I woke and scrambled towards the back window. The sky was red with the breaking dawn, and outside I could see a field full of black and white cows, a chain-link fence and rows of neat, gleaming trailers lined up along a stretch of glistening, black tarmac. Next to each trailer was a brand-new four-by-four heavy-duty car.

Our convoy must have looked monstrous in comparison.

Aunt Minnie and the girls waved at me from the car behind, their cigarettes glowing like sparklers. Frankie's old brown and cream fright was looking more like a rotten tooth than a passable caravan amongst that lot.

I laughed and waved back. At least we were colourful.

We passed by the owner's redbrick house and came into a large clearing filled with trailers, cars, outhouses and children's toys.

We stopped, and I waved for Romaine to come and release me. She slid open the door and clapped her hands. 'Oh, my god, this is so cushti, come and have a look.'

I walked round to the front of the van. Henry-Joe and Jimmy scrambled over our mother's lap, sprinting off toward the grassy island at the camp's centre. Leaping around it were several other children, all dressed like little

china dolls, with perfect ringlets, bell-shaped dresses and
little-old-man suits. The boys, scruffy and unconcerned,
dived over to join them.

A grit lane circled the grassy island, and beyond it stood
a ring of concrete plots, each with its own tap, electric box
and space for two good-sized trailers. Towards the entrance
to the clearing was a large redbrick toilet block with two
saloon-door entrances marked male and female. Beyond
them we could hear the reassuring sound of a working
flush.

Frankie and Aunt Minnie emerged, and lit up fresh cigarettes.

'I've warmed a seat up for you, Bettie,' Aunt Minnie
shouted, nudging Frankie and laughing.

My mother rolled her eyes and laughed.

'Just look at these two tramps will you. The owner's
gonna take one look at those two fools and chuck us straight
off.'

To the side of the camp stood a twenty-foot steel net
and barbed-wire wall, and on the other side there was an
army barrack. We could see, inside a giant shed, heavy
machinery and camouflaged vehicles, with soldiers moving
around them.

The men of the convoy went over to the house to meet
the owner. Most places were filled, but thanks to Rayleen's
family, we were expected and there were four good-sized
plots waiting for us.

As crowds of people started to pour from the other
trailers, I headed in the direction of the wood at the back
end of the camp, hoping to avoid the meet-and-greet
gathering. I planned to have a sly smoke there. I didn't

want to give my father any reason to start on me again, so, unlike Frankie, I kept my smoking a secret.

As I walked away, Aunt Rayleen called me. 'Hey, Mikey, come and meet the boys.'

Shit.

I accelerated into a trot, and dived into the first entrance into the wood that I could see, then waited in silence like a hunted hare as Rayleen called again. After several moments of tensed-up fear, I relaxed, safe for the moment.

I pulled out my cigarette box and lighter.

Looking around I realised that it wasn't actually a real wood. The trees were just a screen to the field behind, which was overgrown and full of battered lorries and scrap.

Just behind the trees was a row of dog kennels, each one housing the favourite dog of the Gypsies – a Lurcher. As I stood, smoking and looking out over the field, I could hear the laughter and chatter from the growing crowd around the convoy. Suddenly I felt like a fool for running away. This was supposed to be my new start and here I was, cowering behind the trees. One of the dogs began to bark at me and, with my cover blown, I headed back into the clearing.

My mother and Rayleen waved as I walked slowly back to join them.

They were standing with three rather odd-looking boys, each with a dramatically different hair colour and build. I guessed that I was about to come face to face with Rayleen's infamous brothers. My first thought was that she had over-sold them in the looks department by a long shot. Despite their different colouring and build, they all looked exactly like her, and she was no oil painting. All four of them had extremely close-set eyes and noses like closed fists. 'Hello there, mate, good to meet you,' they chorused, each shaking my hand.

My father beckoned me over to help, as he pulled Frankie's trailer free from Aunt Minnie's car. Two of the brothers disappeared, but the youngest, Alex, offered to help. My father, purple in the face, heaved at the front of the trailer as we pushed from behind. Once it was settled onto the plot my mother had chosen for us, my father moved on to help Uncle Jaybus and the others before returning to work on the bigger trailer. Alex and I were left winding down the legs of the trailer, and he chatted cheerfully away about the site and the people there.

'I've heard loads about you,' he panted, spinning the trailer jack.

Obviously not, was all I could think, otherwise he wouldn't even be talking to me. I struggled to overcome my shyness.

'Yeah, me too you.'

For the rest of the evening we didn't part company, He even offered to take me for a drive around Newark in his car. It seemed I might make a real friend after all.

As he went off to fetch it, I leaned into the big trailer, where my mother was shooing Henry-Joe and Jimmy out of the toy cupboard.

'I'm going with Alex to the shop, is that all right?'

My mother's face lit up. 'He's a nice boy, isn't he?'

'Yeah, he is.'

She smiled and reached for her handbag. She pulled out

a twenty-pound note and, after looking both ways and whispering 'Shhhhh', she put it in my hand. 'Don't tell your dad, otherwise he'll keep you here to help him set up.'

As we ploughed through the back lanes in Alex's bright red pick-up, we talked about the feud between him and his brothers and the Walsh boys.

Apparently it all stemmed from a row over a girl the year before at the Cambridge Fair; a huge Gypsy convention held every July, where Gypsies from all over the country came together to eat, drink, show off their well-earned motorcars and, of course, fight.

I made it clear to Alex that the feud is nothing to do with me.

'Me neither,' he said, slapping his hand down on the steering wheel.

During the drive around Newark, I learned that Alex was three years older than me, had two different girlfriends who knew nothing of one another, and regularly enjoyed going out on the town to score with Gorgia women.

'Have you had any sorts yet, Mikey?'

I cringed, twitched and muttered a story about a girl in Doncaster.

'What was she like, then?'

I spent the next ten minutes describing what I thought would be a typical sexy yet believable girl, and the ten after that trying to make her sound slightly less of a dog. The look on Alex's face told me that he had guessed I was a virgin. But he politely went along with the story I struggled so hard to come up with.

As we pulled back into the camp, we saw Frankie and

Romaine propped up against the wooden gate with a group of other teenagers. As we got closer, I saw Alex eyeing a girl with long blonde hair and legs about as long as my dumpy sister was tall.

'Now that is a *sort*,' he said.

As we pulled up to the grass verge, the girl turned and stared at us. Alex wound down the window.

'Hello,' she chirped.

Frankie and Romaine squeezed in either side.

'You all right, shit-heads? I'm his sister Frankie by the way.'

The giant girl giggled. 'I'm Kayla-Jayne.'

Two other boys and a girl appeared at the window on my side.

The girl ignored me, and began talking over my shoulder, focusing on the more important, driving teen. She asked Alex about his relationship status and car.

'I'm single, but looking to settle down,' he said, smiling sweetly.

I nearly choked on my can of Coke.

As the girl chatted on I looked at the two boys. They seemed friendly; unlike the usual aggressive boys I had met before. I realised that this was the longest I had ever been in the company of other young people without being challenged to fight. And it felt good.

A little later Alex dropped me back at our trailer and said he would call by later. The big trailer was now settled, with its legs wound down and, just for good measure, my mother was giving it another good scrub to get rid of the dirt from the journey.

All that was left to do was to attach the awning to the

front of it and I had come back just in time to help. Many
of the trailers had awnings attached to the sides, but my
mother, who couldn't help but bring her Elton John decor
taste into everything, had had an awning made especially
to fit the whole front of the trailer, like a passion-pink
circus tent; frills and all. Even though the night air had
already begun to draw in, my father was determined to get
the job over and done with. The great pink lump, along
with its one hundred-plus attachment poles had been pulled
from its sack and spread across the concrete to let the
creases fall out. This monstrosity of a contraption was my
least favourite part of the set up, mainly because it always
caused my father to blow his fuse. Not once had it been
attached without me or one of my brothers being whacked
with the one pole that never fitted.

For several of our moves we had made do without it,
since it was such a nightmare to assemble, but now we
were planning to stay a while, and my mother wanted it
up.

A group of teenagers had assembled in Frankie's trailer,
and they watched as my father wrestled with the awning,
shouted, sulked and swore for the next couple of hours.
What seemed like an eternity later, it was done. My father
managed to crack me a smile as we stood back to admire
our handiwork.

'Come and have a look, Bettie.'

My mother descended from the trailer and out through
the zip door of her creation to join us.

'You happy?' my father said proudly, pulling her to him
with a kiss.

She leaned into his chest and looked over at the finished

object, tilting her head. She gave a half-pleased hum, and that was good enough for me. I made a dash for it and joined Frankie and the others in her trailer.

For the first time, I began to feel confident around others my age. Alex soon joined us, and we all sat around, talking and smoking.

The two teenage boys who'd hung around the car earlier were there, and Alex began to taunt them. 'What are your names then, Little and Large?'

It was cruel, but accurate. They got up and made polite excuses to leave.

'Wanna come and play pool, Mikey?' asked the thinner boy.

'Not with you he don't,' laughed Alex.

As the boys left I couldn't help but feel sorry for them. They reminded me of myself.

I went outside to say goodbye to them. The three of us stood awkwardly, listening to Alex and Frankie back in the trailer, firing off insults about them and screaming with laughter.

'I'll see you later, thanks for coming up.' I spoke loudly, trying to drown out the noise behind me.

The two boys looked up to the window, as Alex waved like the Queen.

'Ignore him.'

The large boy walked off, rubbing his face in a temper.

The smaller one shook my hand. 'I'm Adam. Your cousin.'

'Really?'

'Yeah, my dad and your dad are first cousins. That makes us second.'

'I never knew that.'

He smiled, then set off after the other boy.

'See you later, cousin,' I called.

'See you later!'

'That wasn't very nice, Alex,' I said, when I was back inside the trailer.

'No it wasn't,' said Romaine. 'I don't know why you're laughing, Frankie.'

'Oh, they were arseholes,' Frankie retorted, laughing her head off.

It was clear that Alex was my stubby little sister's type. I knew she would never act that way if she didn't fancy him.

'Why are you laughing like that?' I said. 'We've been here two minutes and you're acting like a bitch.'

She paused. 'Oh shut up, Joseph, who are you to tell me off like a child?'

'What did you call me?'

She snickered, wiping the mascara that had run down her cheeks and pulling herself up from Alex's shoulder.

'Joseph . . . Joseph, Joseph, Joseph, Joseph, Joseph, Joseph, *Joseph*!'

I put my outstretched arm behind her music system.

She screamed. 'Don't you dare!'

I launched the thing off the table, sending it exploding into a wall before it crashed to the carpet and splattered across the floor. Then I got up and walked out.

The trailer door flew open and Frankie's shrill voice echoed throughout the camp. 'Fucking poof! Fucking poofy boy! Beat rotten by every, fucking low-life man that's ever faced you! Hey, everybody, my brother is a big poof! A big, man-loving *poof*! *And now you all know*!'

She slammed the trailer door so hard it sent a shock-wave across the camp.

As the echoes faded, so did my hope for change.

19

The Wrath of Frankie

In the days that followed my father found a local quarry where we could get tar and grit, and an abundance of unsuspecting victims. He and I would leave the camp for the quarry every morning at 6 a.m. and only after shifting the majority of our cargo onto the drives of local pensioners for ridiculous amounts of money, or when it had become too dark to work, did we head back home.

I was glad, because every time I stepped back into Frankie's trailer, I revisited her humiliating outburst. The other teenagers would be gathered there, but although I was included, things were not the same. Frankie's bellow across the camp had truly stuck, and the brief moment in which I had felt what it was like to be a normal, popular kid was gone.

Frankie was too stubborn a girl to admit to anyone, including me, that she had been wrong, and it drove yet another wedge between us, because I found it hard to forgive her.

Alex was still friendly with me, but I suspected that it was because I was his excuse to come over to the trailer every evening. Frankie had made our trailer the new teenage girl hangout, and there was no better place for any red-blooded teenage Gypsy boy to be. Sitting with Frankie would be Romaine, now a giggly twelve-year-old, Kayla-Jayne, the chatty girl who'd stuck her head in at the car window, and her buck-toothed sister Charlene.

The two boys who had been mocked that first evening – our second cousins Adam and Levoy – often hung around, and through their sheer persistence, were gradually accepted by Alex and became part of the group.

The two of them looked a bit like Laurel and Hardy. Adam was rake thin, with bow legs and the slight look of a chimpanzee around the ears. Levoy was double the size of little Adam, and the perfect comic relief. Although he had slightly more of a darker side to his personality than Adam it didn't often surface until suddenly he'd hit you with a quip that would tear you apart. Levoy adored Adam, the two of them were inseparable, and secretly I shared his admiration; I thought Adam was amazing.

Once the girls had finished their daily cleaning chores, they would all come in and Frankie would pull the blinds. There they would sit for hours, smoking sneaky cigarettes, talking 'women's troubles' and gossiping about boys. Or so we boys assumed. Sometimes the four of us – me, Alex, Adam and Levoy – tried to listen outside the window, to find out what they talked about. We were shocked, one evening, to hear one of the girls screaming in panic over having accidentally lost her virginity to a tampon. The girls all screeched and fussed as the four of us rolled about in the grass in stitches. I learned that night yet another secret rule of the dos and don'ts of the Gypsy girls' code: they were not supposed to use tampons in case they broke the hymen before their wedding night.

All the girls fancied Alex, and when he arrived they would try to outdo themselves in giggling and flirting with him, while squabbling openly about who he liked best. Listening from outside as I climbed the steps after work, I felt embarrassed for them. Worst of all was my sister, who put on a laugh that she clearly thought was adorable, but which in fact sounded painfully fake and very Wicked Witch of the West.

I grew up thinking that the girls had it easy. But as we all reached teenage, I began to see just how much pressure was on them. The dread that they might not marry before they were eighteen, and might have to join the ranks of the spinsters must have been awful. Once they hit twenty, their chance of ever having a family was virtually over. Only a rare few ever married after that age.

One evening I stepped into the trailer to find Frankie sitting on Alex's lap, play-fighting over a carton of cigarettes. Seeing me, Alex peeled her off and leaped up, protesting that he'd been waiting for me. We both knew that, as her brother, I should be defending Frankie's honour by punching Alex's lights out. But I had no intention of doing that. All I wanted was to shower out of my hair the hideous pink dust from the grit I'd shovelled all day.

After packing a bag and prising Alex away from the girls, we set off for the local sports centre for a shower, as the one at the camp, having been smashed up three times by a phantom shower-head smasher, was now permanently out of action because the owner refused to fix it again. As he drove, Alex clearly felt the need to explain himself.

'I wasn't just up there to see her, I was waiting for you,' he said.

'That's nice, Alex.'

'Ain't you upset or nothing?'

'No.'

'Why not?'

'I don't care about her having boys up the trailer to visit,' I told him. 'It's not as if you were on your own with her. But if you think it's wrong, don't expect me to take your head off, just stop going up there. Frankie's big and ugly enough to look after herself.'

Alex looked shocked. I felt he would have preferred a good smack.

When we reached the sports centre, the showers were packed. I hated having to go to public showers, and always kept shorts on, but Alex used the shower as an opportunity to celebrate the prowess of his rather smaller than average cock.

'This may be a small one,' he'd say, 'but it's had more sorts than any man in this room.'

No one but Alex could be vain enough to introduce his prick to a room full of people, and yet simultaneously try to start a fight about it at the same time.

I kept my mouth shut and kept on scrubbing. I wasn't bailing him out of a fight until I was good and clean.

Thankfully he got away with it, and after our shower we headed back to the camp, to find the others still sitting around exactly as we'd left them. We spent the evening smoking and talking about who was getting married, who had a nice car, who was a whore and who was dead, while listening to Frankie's Prince and Michael Jackson tape mix playing over and over again.

Glad as I was to be part of a group, it could be stifling at times. So when Alex asked me if I'd like to go to Brighton with him to visit one of his girlfriends, I leaped at the chance.

For the first time my father was actually paying me for my labours. Until now he'd insisted it should be me paying him for the experience of working with him, but for a week now he had paid me ten pounds a day, so I had some money of my own.

Alex had been disappearing for weekends over the past few months, but we never knew where he went. I didn't mind, because I spent that time with Adam and Levoy, and found them easy company. Unlike Alex, they seldom talked about girls, being far less confident or experienced than he was, and that suited me. I felt easy and relaxed with them. But I was flattered to be let in on Alex's secret and to join in an adventure with him. We booked a travel inn close to the camp where his girl lived, and on Saturday morning we set off. On the long drive down, we talked about all the usual Gypsy boy things: girls, marriage and of course fighting – who had beaten who, where and how badly. I wasn't really interested, but I knew the drill.

Eventually we lapsed into silence until, in a small voice, Alex said, 'I was scared to death when you first arrived – I thought you were gonna smash my face in.'

'You can't have heard much about me then.'

'Do you wanna know something else?' he continued. 'I'm scared that now you're living in Newark, your cousins will come up to visit and beat the shit out of me and my brothers.'

I laughed. I knew Uncle Tory's family would never set foot out of their own territory. 'I wouldn't worry about that, Alex.'

He paused, and then said, 'Do you ever wish that you had been someone else?'

It was as if he had just read my mind, but I didn't dare to say so. 'No,' I told him, lighting a cigarette.

But he was on a roll, and carried on. 'I've had a few fights, but I ain't worth two shits. I've hid in a cupboard more than I've put my hands up – you ever done that?'

'I'm not allowed to, Alex.'

'So you've had to fight every man that's come to your door?'

'Yes.'

'Won any?'

'No.'

'Bet that hasn't gone down well with your dad and Uncle Tory. My father would rather I hide away. He would do anything to keep out of trouble. Anyway, I'm a lover not a fighter.'

I felt exactly the same way. But I couldn't let him see that. If I had learned anything, it was not to open up. I had far too much to hide to be able to be as honest with him as he was being with me. I envied him. I wished my father would have let me hide in a cupboard.

Once we got to Brighton we checked into our hotel and went off to meet his girl at a McDonalds in the town centre. When we arrived she was already there, a buxom, dark-haired girl who threw her arms around Alex as soon as she saw him. What Alex hadn't told me was that she was bringing a friend for me, Jenny, a tiny girl of fourteen, covered in slap and wearing a pair of heels that seemed twice the size of her actual feet.

I was horrified, but there was nothing I could do but play along. We moved on to a bar and when Alex and I went up to get the drinks, he nudged me and asked me what I thought of her.

I told him she wasn't my type. But Alex laughed. 'Mikey, you're only here for one night, you might as well try and get something out of this trip.'

He was right. If she liked me, it would be a heaven-sent opportunity to land myself a girlfriend.

Half an hour later Alex and his girl left, winking at us as they went. The other girl and I sat and struggled to make awkward small talk. After a bit she moved closer to me, running her fingers through her hair and pouting.

She sighed, 'I wish I had a boyfriend.'

Like all Gypsy girls, she couldn't ask a boy out, so she had to drop a hefty hint. I certainly couldn't kiss her unless we were 'going out'.

I turned to her and said it. 'Will you go out with me?'

'Yes,' she cooed, and without pausing she pounced on me for my first-ever kiss.

I could taste her lipstick, mingled with Big Mac. I opened my eyes, looked into her heavily made-up face – and panicked. Having a girlfriend meant calling her every day, buying her presents, paying for everything, and if I couldn't make her hate me enough to dump me after a few months, I'd have to propose.

For the rest of the afternoon we walked around Brighton, stopping to kiss every few minutes. Not because I wanted to, but because I could think of absolutely nothing to say to her. I was overjoyed when Alex rejoined us and we headed back to the hotel.

The next morning, on the way back to Newark, Alex spoke to his girl on the phone. 'Mikey, Jenny told my girl to say you're finished.'

A burden lifted from my shoulders. What a piece of luck to have met the one Gypsy girl in the country who just wanted a bit of fun. Or perhaps it was the fact that I showed no real interest in her, and kissed her as if I was sucking on a lemon.

A week later, Jay got into trouble with the police and the family had to leave. Alex said he would come back to visit. But he never did.

I missed him, but at least Frankie and I were getting on better. One evening the two of us dressed Henry-Joe and Jimmy up as hookers and sent them over to Aunt Minnie's to borrow a cigarette. We watched through the window, both of us in stitches, as they waddled over in Frankie's high heels. Henry-Joe and Jimmy had become as inseparable as Frankie and I had been at their age. Wherever Henry-Joe was, Jimmy was never more than a few feet behind. They only parted when Jimmy was training. He'd been jogging round the camp and weight-lifting since he was four, and at five my father began sparring with him. I noticed that my father's approach had become less brutal, though he would never admit that he was too harsh with me. In fact, he used my failure to spur Jimmy on. I'd be cleaning the car outside and I'd hear my father taunting, 'Harder, come on!'

Jimmy would grunt like a little pig as he punched my father's palms.

'Harder! Do you want to end up like "Nancy Anne" over there?'

After years of put-downs I had learned to ignore it. It was only when Adam and Levoy were around that it was humiliating. I'd explain that it was my father's sense of humour. He was still ripping me apart and beating me in front of the dossas at work for being too weak, too slow and too stupid. And apart from Adam and Levoy, I couldn't say my name to a man within ten years of my age without being asked to fight and getting my head kicked in, then being publicly beaten by my father for losing.

I hated myself. I was useless. I was a stupid coward who couldn't fight to save his life; I couldn't even handle a shovel at work.

But there was something even worse. I had a secret that would surely one day destroy me, and my family too.

Every night, I would climb into my bunk and lie awake, thinking about what I was going to do. How was I going to get out of this place before it was too late? It was only a matter of time before they would all see through me. The rumours were already spreading like poison, triggered by Frankie's outburst. I needed to prove myself, but the only way would be to find a girl and marry her, and my six-hour fling with Jenny had convinced me I was never going to be able do that.

I was trapped. I didn't know a thing about life beyond this camp. I had no education, no money and no way to survive on my own.

Yet to stay might be even worse.

20

Sex Education

It was while we were at Newark that my mother gave birth to her fifth and last child – a little girl she named Minnie, after her favourite sister. Born as a complete surprise to all of us, including our mother, Minnie was black-haired and dark-eyed and we all doted on her, though I seldom got to see much of her, because my father kept me busy most waking hours.

He had a new job for me. Sick of driving his lorry down cul-de-sacs, then spending ages struggling to get back out of them again, he decided that it would look more professional to go knocking on doors using the transit van, with the lorry on standby around the corner. It was time I got my driving licence.

My mother picked up an application for a provisional licence from the post office and, that night, my father took it with him to the pub, where he got the landlord to help him fill it out correctly.

At that time a provisional licence could be requested without having to send off a birth certificate, so he added four years to my age, sent the form off and a couple of weeks later the licence arrived.

I began taking lessons right away – two a week at ten pounds a go, from an old guy called Jack. He was a regular at the Gypsies' local, and made a lot of money by teaching practically every teenage Gypsy in the camp while turning a blind eye to their real ages.

I failed my first test miserably, by taking the wing mirror off a passing car, failed my second without even getting into the lorry, having left my provisional licence at home, but third time around, I scraped a pass with an instructor who spent most of the test on the phone to his wife.

I was only thirteen, but we were all old before our time. That's the way we lived.

A childhood for any Gypsy was very short indeed.

It was around the same time that it was decided that it was time for me to be introduced to sex. Just because Gypsy girls had to be chaste, it didn't mean that the boys were going to be. Most of them tended to frequent prostitutes to relieve their sexual frustration, unless they won the jackpot of finding a Gorgia girl who would oblige for free.

There were a surprising number of willing girls around, and the Gypsy boys were quick to respond. Their pockets, their fists and their cocks were all that mattered. They hunted in groups; making it an outing for the lads.

'Old, So-'n'-So's boy's still a virgin, let's take him out, get him fucked, and we'll all make a day of it.'

It was kind of like that.

My initiation into manhood was to take place down at the local Dyna Bowl, where a group of us teenagers tended to hang out in the evenings. One of the older boys in the camp, Colbert Runt, had found a couple of Gorgia girls who had agreed to meet us for drinks and some 'no strings' sex.

My choice, laughed Colbert, was known as 'Gobbler'. It seemed her friends had given her the nickname because she was able to fit her whole fist inside her baby maker.

And word was she'd have sex with anything that moved. My heart sank.

Once again I had to prove myself as a man. Only this time it was not in a ring, but in the back of an old van, with a girl who sounded like my idea of a nightmare. Either I slept with her, or went home with my reputation even more tattered than it already was.

Those rumours, fuelled by Frankie's outburst when we first arrived in Newark, had never gone away. My mother said it was because I was too pretty to be a boy, which was of no comfort whatsoever, and my father quite openly referred to me in public as Nancy Anne.

Luckily for me, Adam and Levoy were coming along to be initiated that night too, by Gobbler's Gypsy-loving friend Tracey. The three of us had frequently bragged about our sexual experiences, while watching *Star Wars* marathons in Levoy's trailer. But now, with Colbert Runt demanding we come on his 'free sex for all' evening, we had to either face up to our lies and confess our lack of carnal knowledge, blag our way through it and hope for the best, or do what any sensible person would do and just say no to the whole stupid idea. Except that to say no would be taken to mean that we couldn't be interested in women, and word would spread like lightning around the camp and beyond.

Adam, Levoy and I all went for the safest option: blag it and hope for the best.

That evening the three of us sat at a table in the Dyna Bowl bar. The ice in our Diet Cokes rattled as we held the glasses to our lips.

Then Colbert and the girls arrived. One looked like a

walrus in a miniskirt, the other like a transvestite in hysterectomy pants. With a 'cooeee' they plonked themselves down next to us. The walrus made a beeline for me.

'Ooh, look at your eyes – hey Tracey, have a look at this one's eyes, they're like sequins, ain't they?'

This had to be Gobbler. Her oversized face was thickly coated in a dark brown foundation, with orange lipstick smudged up onto her nose.

'You've scored with that one, Mikey,' chuckled Adam, but the laughter soon disappeared from his face as Tracey swooped in and squeezed herself between him and Levoy, placing a meaty hand firmly on his thigh.

After a few minutes of desultory chatter, Tracey grabbed Adam and Levoy and headed off. Gobbler followed suit, grabbing me by the hand and leading me outside and round to the back steps behind the Dyna Bowl. It wasn't exactly a romantic setting. The air was like ice, and the steps were clearly more often used as a urinal than anything else. Gobbler sucked brutally on my tongue, tearing at my belt and raising her legs about my waist. I reciprocated reluctantly as she fumbled with her tights, ripping them down then pulling my hand into the crotch of her knickers.

I kept thinking of Adam and Levoy with Tracey and wondering if they'd managed to go through with it. I smacked her hand away as she made a swipe for my uninterested nether regions.

'The condoms, get the condoms,' she groaned.

Thank God! I thought; she had just handed me a golden excuse to get the hell out of there.

'I forgot to bring one,' I muttered, leaping off her. 'I've got to get one off of Adam.'

'Go then,' she panted. 'Don't keep me waiting here with me legs open.'

I zipped up, running back round to the front of the Bowl as if my life depended on it. There was absolutely no way I was going back around that corner, and I pitied anyone who might have stumbled around there for a drunken piss in the next few minutes.

Luckily for me I had held out for longer than Adam and Levoy had. They were sitting back at the table with Colbert, gulping on a fresh drink when I went back inside. They all looked at me.

'So,' said Colbert. 'Did you fuck her, or what?'

I'd already planned this part. 'No way, she's dirty.'

'Yeah, ours was too, wasn't she Levoy?' said Adam.

'Er, yeah,' muttered Levoy finally catching on.

It wasn't much of an excuse, but Colbert wasn't the brightest spark and didn't ask questions.

'Oh well, he smirked. 'Plenty more where that came from.'

I prayed not.

We downed our drinks and left the Bowl before Gobbler and Tracey reappeared. Back at the camp, Adam, Levoy and I headed for Levoy's trailer. We spent the rest of the evening making up stories about how great the girls had been at giving head.

Levoy and Adam passed their driving tests within a month of each other and as a reward Adam was given a new BMW and Levoy a brand-new Toyota van. Every night, just as my father would go from trailer to trailer to call for the men, Levoy would call for us teenagers. One by one we would stack ourselves into the back of his van, but only after a good twenty-minute argument between the girls about who would get to sit in the front. Kayla-Jane and Frankie always won, so Romaine and Charlene were always in the back with me and Adam.

We still went to the Dyna-Bowl, because it was one of the few places in town that we could hang out. As soon as we arrived in the car park we would head straight to the bar where all of us, including Levoy, would get wasted on diamond white cider and jelly shots. My father had stopped paying me while I was learning to drive the lorry, and afterwards reinstated my wages at just twenty pounds a week. But my mother would give me extra without my father knowing. Like the other boys, I would blow the lot on drinks and cigarettes at the Dyna Bowl bar.

With our group – Frankie, Kayla-Jane, Adam, Levoy, Romaine and Charlene – I felt at my most comfortable. We would play drinking games, and torment Adam and Romaine who had started going out with each other. There were still rules – we boys had to pay for the girls, no mention of sex words and so on, but it was the nearest I ever got to really relaxing.

Sometimes, to change the pace, we'd go to the cinema. One night the others in the group voted to see *The Lion King* for the third time. I decided to give it a miss. With the cinema being next to the Dyna Bowl, I bought a packet of cigarettes, told the others I'd see them later, and headed over to the bar on my own.

'What can I get you, mate?'

I had noticed this particular barman several times before. He had a warm smile, bright blue eyes and tattooed arms.

'We've got a two-for-one offer on Fosters if you fancy it?'

'All right then, I'll have two of them.'

I sat at a high stool at the bar as he poured. I took a sip. I'd never tasted lager before. It was so rancid I nearly spat it out, but I had to keep some kind of composure in front of the barman.

'You're one of the travelling lot aren't you?'

'Yeah,' I answered suspiciously.

'The travellers have always lived around here. I live just up the road from the campsite. Always thought you lot were all right.'

I took another swig of the lager. 'Do you wanna help me finish the other one?'

He smiled again. 'Thanks. I'm finished now, I'll just get my coat.'

While he was gone the danger of what I was doing hit me. I was about to share a beer and conversation with a Gorgia man. My father – not to mention the rest of the men back at the camp – would probably kill me if they found out.

Kayla-Jayne and Charlene's older sister Esther, a pretty girl of twenty, once told me that she used to hang around this same bar with two other Gypsy girls. One of them had started seeing a Gorgia man, and when their fathers found out, all three were not only banned from ever going there again, but were labelled whores, which meant not one of them would ever marry. It was a terrible punishment, and now here I was, risking even worse. But I felt excited by the idea of talking to someone new, someone outside our small, closed world.

He appeared a minute later and sat on the stool next to

me. His name was Caleb, he was twenty-five years old and he'd been working in the bar since dropping out of the Navy two years before.

'I'm Mikey,' I told him, 'and I'm nineteen.'

You weren't even supposed to be in the bar until you were eighteen. I'd added one for luck.

We talked for a while, then he looked at his watch. 'I have to shoot off, do you want to come for a drink with me and some friends?

'I can't, I've got to get back.'

Our chat had lasted all of twenty minutes. I waited for him to leave the building before I left for the cinema. I felt guilty for breaking the rules. But I wished I could have gone with him.

In the weeks that followed I saw Caleb whenever I went into the bar with the others. He was always friendly when I went over to order drinks, and several times he repeated his invitation to go out with him and his friends. But I didn't dare accept.

Then everything changed. A new group of Gypsy boys, from a campsite a few miles away, heard about the Dyna Bowl hangout and arrived one night to see for themselves.

I was drunk and doing impressions of Aunt Minnie, when three stocky, greased-up Gypsy boys entered the bar. Without any introduction, they bought their drinks, came right over to our table and took a seat. They closed in, blatantly chatting up the girls while giving Adam, Levoy and me the cold shoulder.

We went out into the lobby to play the fruit machines and discuss the situation.

'It's all gonna change now,' said Levoy in a morbid tone.

'Why?' I asked.

'Because now this lot know we all come here we won't get rid of them,' said Adam.

'Who are they?'

Adam and Levoy knew of them and gave me the low down on the newcomers. They said that the group had been banned from the main Gypsy haunt a few miles away, after countless violent attacks on Gorgias and other Gypsies.

Romaine came out to join us. 'I think your sister's found a man in there, Mikey.'

'What!'

'Yep, he's already buying them drinks and flirting.'

I went over to the door to see. Sure enough, Kayla-Jayne, Frankie and even sour-faced Charlene were melting and giggling at every word that came out of the boys' mouths.

Then I heard Frankie's wicked witch laugh. Romaine was right.

I walked through the bar and into the toilet, where I composed myself before making my way back to the table. Adam and Romaine had already returned, but were sitting outside of the intimate circle the girls had formed with the new boys. But Levoy was doing his best to get friendly, and appeared to be succeeding.

'This is my brother,' Frankie said.

Davey Nelson took one look, then leaned over to Levoy and the other boys and whispered. The three of them let out a laugh, and the sound of Levoy joining in crushed me. He was an even bigger coward than I was.

The boy interested in Frankie, wanting to impress her, rose from his seat and gave me a heavy handshake.

'How yer doin, mush. Me name's Wisdom, this is Davey, and this is Tyrone.'

He turned back to Frankie. I didn't even bother sitting down.

Romaine tapped Adam on the leg, gave me a nod and the three of us left.

Adam flagged down a taxi. 'You gonna head home with us, Mikey?'

I wished I could, but I wasn't about to leave my sister. 'Na, it's all right, I'll see you when we get back.'

I went back inside and sat in silence as Frankie and the other girls lapped up the attention for the next two hours. Finally we made our way back to the camp with the new boys in tow. I realised that Levoy had been right: everything was going to change, and I was furious that these boys could walk in and destroy it all.

When we pulled back into the camp, I jumped out and went straight back to our trailer. I was in no mood to sit in the car park, watching the girls and Levoy humiliate themselves by going cock-eyed over a bunch of apes.

After that night, the new boys became a regular fixture, and they brought other friends with them. Before long Frankie began dating Wisdom, Kayla-Jayne got together with Tyrone and Charlene pulled the leader, Davey.

Most painful of all to Adam and me was that Levoy had chosen to join them too. He stopped coming for me in the evening, and when he saw me, he turned the other way.

In a matter of weeks, our group had shrunk to just Adam, Romaine and me.

One evening Adam came to call.

'Come on out, Mikey, the three of us can have a laugh. We can ignore all of them. Besides, it's Romaine's thirteenth.'

Our mouths dropped open in shock as we reached the Dyna Bowl car park and saw the sea of transit vans and pick-ups.

Inside the bar was a mass gathering of Gypsy youth. Frankie spotted me. 'Oi, get me a diamond white and black,' she called.

I asked Adam and Romaine what they wanted and headed for the bar.

Caleb was there. 'Your lot are certainly packing in these days,' he said.

'I know,' I said with a sigh.

I watched him laughing with the rest of the staff as he poured our drinks. What I wouldn't give just to be normal. To be able to work in a pub, wear a silly bowling shirt and cap and just serve drinks for the rest of my life.

As I walked over to give Frankie her drink there was a loud 'wooooo'. I had been spotted chatting to the barman, and to these people that meant something sick or gay. As they laughed and jeered, I picked up my drink and walked away.

Romaine grabbed my arm. 'Don't leave, Mikey,' she pleaded. 'You'll only make it worse.'

'Just sit down here with us,' said Adam, 'we'll stay for a drink and then we'll go.'

But I couldn't bear it in there any longer. I walked out of the building and round to the back. After smoking a couple of cigarettes, I headed back to the entrance, hoping that Adam and Romaine would be waiting for me and we could go home.

They weren't, but others were.

As I got closer I heard Colbert Runt whisper, 'There he is coming now.'

I knew what was coming. Just like Levoy, Colbert had joined the new boys to take me down for fun.

'Oi, poofy boy.' A fat-headed thug stepped out from a group that had gathered in front of the door. I kept my head down and tried stepping around him. He pushed me backwards. 'You're Frank Walsh's boy?'

'Yes,' I replied.

'I bet he punched your mother up something good for popping you out.'

The others cheered as he rushed forward to punch me. But it was clear he had never learned to box; his face was fully exposed. I drew back my fist and punched him as hard as I could on the bridge of his nose. As he fell, face first, to the floor, the others rushed towards me in a stampede. Two boys grabbed hold of my arms, and while the thug got back to his feet and punched my ribs and stomach, Colbert Runt turned his gold rings to the jagged edge, punching me over and over on my forehead face and nose.

Rage ran through me as blood poured from my face.

I could hear Frankie and the girls screaming and the punches kept coming. They had all heard the fight and come outside to see. Then two security men and Caleb pulled me free of the gang and took me inside.

Frankie, Adam and Romaine stood in the doorway as I went by. I asked Adam if he could get them home right away.

'Will you be all right?' he asked.

'I'll be all right.'

Caleb helped me up to the staff toilet and sat me down. He handed me a damp cloth, then stood quietly, going through a first-aid box, as I swore, shouted and punched at the walls.

I looked into the mirror. There were three gaping cuts on my face; the worst of them right down the bridge of my nose. At the sight of my face my anger turned to panic. My father was going to kill me for getting beaten up.

'I think I need stitches.'

Caleb began cutting off strips of tape. 'Have a seat, I'll have a go at closing them.'

I sat quietly as Caleb dabbed the strips of tape across my face.

'This is what we really are. Do you still think we're a good lot, Caleb?'

'I suppose not,' he replied. 'But there's still one good one I know of, only I can't get him to come out for a beer with me.'

I laughed. 'Well, I'm officially hated now, mate, so I don't think you'll be seeing much of me any more.'

'If you're hated, then they won't have much to do with your time, will they?'

I explained to Caleb that for me to go out with him and his buddies for a drink would be impossible. 'We're not allowed to mix with people who aren't Gypsies.'

'Well, don't tell 'em then.' He gave a cheeky smile. 'I've just finished work, they've all gone, so how about it?'

I took a look in the mirror. He'd done such a good job that I almost looked as if I hadn't just had the crap beaten out of me twenty minutes before. If there was ever to be a chance for me to see him, then this was it.

'OK then.'

He checked that the coast was clear as we walked out to his car: a little orange Micra that looked like a little rusted pumpkin.

As we drove, my stomach did somersaults. I began laughing. I couldn't believe what I was doing; I was sitting in a Gorgia car with a Gorgia man, who was taking me to the Gorgia pub for a drink.

He took me to a typical little English pub, with low wooden beams and copper pots hanging on the walls. It was well away from the Dyna Bowl, and had lots of dark corners where I could sit without feeling self-conscious about my wounds.

Caleb got us drinks and began asking me about my life. From there the conversation just flowed. It was wonderful to be able to talk about something other than money, fighting and girls.

When I had finished, Caleb told me about his school, his college and his brief Navy life, as well as his friends, his girlfriends and his family. He was the first genuinely happy person I had ever met. All that mattered were his family, his friends and enjoying his life.

When it came to my turn I couldn't stop talking. I had never felt so free to talk about myself. I told him things I had never told anyone before: about my father, the fighting, and the rules of Gypsy life.

I left three things out: Joseph, being gay, and my real age. I didn't know him well enough to trust him with any of those secrets.

When last orders were called I knew I would have to face going back and showing myself to my father. Caleb drove me back, and I asked him to pull into the park next door to our camp, in case we were seen. The place next door was a council-owned trailer park for permanent residents, all of them elderly Gorgias.

He turned off the engine and we pushed back our seats and talked in the dark.

He told me about his favourite music, his love of motorbikes and how he one day hoped to get promoted to manager of the whole Dyna Bowl.

'I'm going out with some mates tomorrow if you wanna come,' he said.

They were going to a nightclub. I had never been to one before.

'Do you think your friends would mind?'

'No. I think they'd really like you.'

I smiled at the idea that anyone might actually like me. I wanted to go, but did I dare? I could risk it. My parents would just assume I was out with the group.

'All right.'

Caleb smiled. 'Shall I pick you up here, then?'

'Yes. That would be great. Can you make it nine?' I knew that by that time Levoy, Frankie and the gang, plus my father, would have left the camp.

'Fine,' he said.

I stood, waiting until his car was out of sight, before I started walking back.

21

Caleb's Plan

I walked back to the camp thinking about Caleb and how much I had enjoyed just being with him. I couldn't wait for the next evening. I would be taking an even bigger risk, but it was worth it. Then I turned a corner – and saw the orange glow of a cigarette. My father was waiting for me. But a filthy look, a dictionary of hateful words and a good kick up the arse barely touched me. I dusted myself off, climbed into the trailer, got undressed and fell into my bunk. I pulled the curtain across and stared up through the open skylight. The stars made me think of Kenny and where he was now. Something important had happened this evening. I had seen a chink of light in the darkness and I was determined not to lose sight of it.

The next evening, once Frankie and the others had gone out and my father was in the pub, I slipped away to meet Caleb. He took me to meet his friends – two girls who also worked at the Dyna Bowl, and a boy who was an old schoolfriend of his. They welcomed me, and I had a really good time. No pressure to fight, or boast, or chase girls, just a friendly evening full of laughter and chatter. I was astounded by the way boys and girls could be friends without any kind of romantic pressure. And how both girls and boys could talk openly about sex.

Over the next few weeks I managed to sneak out to meet

Caleb nearly every night. Sometimes we met with his friends, other times it was just the two of us. It was surprisingly easy to slip out of the camp. By this time, few of the others my age wanted to hang around with me; I was social poison to the boys and a lost cause to the girls. Only Adam and Romaine still offered to go out with me, but I told them I didn't feel like going anywhere. And then, a few weeks later, Adam suddenly left the camp. He was shipped off to run a place his father had bought in Scotland, but the real reason was that his family didn't approve of Romaine. His family were very well off, and considered Aunt Minnie and her family common. Aunt Minnie swore, chain-smoked, drank, and didn't give a shit what anyone thought of her. Uncle Jaybus, was exactly the same, and so was Romaine, who had a straggly ponytail, wore three-inch thick layers of make-up and a gaudy selection of 'designer' tracksuits.

Romaine was crushed, but eventually she began hanging around with another girl at the camp.

I was sorry, because I really liked Adam. But after he left, it was even simpler for me to slip away to meet Caleb.

After work each day – we got back anywhere between two and six each afternoon, depending on the job in hand – I went in to sit with my mother, the boys and Minnie until Frankie was up and ready, around six. My father would be out talking to the men or collecting more tarmac and I would chat to my mother, help the boys with their games, and give Minnie a cuddle.

Once Frankie was up I would go back to our trailer, get a bowl of hot water and wash the pink dust off me. Levoy would arrive to collect Frankie and Kayla-Jayne and around seven my father would drive around the camp collecting all the men to go to the pub.

I was grateful that my father didn't ask me to drive the men to the pub any more. A few months earlier, not long after passing my test, I had crashed my father's car head on with another car on a main road. I had taken Romaine and Frankie to buy cigarettes, it was raining and I came off a roundabout and lost control. None of us were hurt, but Frankie had to call my father to come down and bribe the driver of the other car, because I wasn't insured. My father persuaded him to pretend it was my mother who crashed into him so that he could get his payout. After that I was beaten soundly and banned from driving.

I would lie low until they'd all gone, so that my parents thought I had gone out with the other teenagers. After they had all left, I would make my way quietly down to the retirement camp to meet Caleb.

After each night out, Caleb and I would end up walking the empty streets of the town, holding each other up and not wanting the night to end. And Caleb would pull me in close and tell me that he loved me. But I couldn't help but think that this might be just how Gorgias are: more open about feelings, not afraid to show affection, and express themselves in ways that my lot never could. So I didn't respond.

The next day Caleb would reassure me that he said it to all his friends when he was pissed, confirming what I had thought. I felt relieved that I hadn't made a fool of myself by telling him I loved him too, even though I knew that I did.

My fourteenth birthday fell on a Saturday and I got a

bus into town and spent the whole day celebrating it with Caleb in an Irish pub. I felt awful every time he raised his glass to me being twenty.

It was nearly 2 a.m. and we were walking home, when he said it again.

'I love you, Mikey.'

I laughed. 'I know, Caleb, you say it all the time.'

He became more serious. 'Don't you believe me?'

'Of course I do,' I answered, 'but you've already said that you say that all the time to your friends.'

Caleb stopped, and faced me. 'Mikey, I love you. I've loved you since I first saw you in the Dyna Bowl.'

'I love you too,' I said. I wrapped my arms around him and held onto him as tightly as I had always dreamed of doing. I could hardly believe that he felt the same way I did.

I couldn't hold back the tears. He joked with me, calling me a big poof, and I laughed. I wished I could tell him just how much this meant to me, and how desperately I had been searching for him all these years.

It was after 3 a.m. when I got back to the retirement camp in a taxi. I walked towards our camp, dazed with happiness and disbelief. Then, from the direction of the toilets I heard a loud 'Oi'.

Frankie and Kayla-Jane were calling from Wisdom's van. I walked over to find Frankie sitting on Wisdom's lap, and Kayla-Jayne on Tyrone's. They were laughing hysterically. As the window wound down, a cloud of marijuana smoke wafted out.

Frankie looked haggard. It had been a good month since I had actually seen her out of bed and conscious. She was asleep when I got up for work each morning, and would leave soon after I got back.

Clearly I wasn't the only one sneaking away at night. The girls had a ten o'clock curfew, but the boys would drop them back, then wait in the van in a nearby field. Once the men of the camp had returned from the pub, the girls would sneak out again to meet them. The discovery of such goings on could ruin their lives. The Gypsies on our camp disliked boys like Davey, Wisdom and Tyrone because they were rough, drug-taking types who gave Gypsies a bad name. Our father, and Kayla-Jayne's, would have a fit if they knew the girls were seeing these boys, let alone sneaking off to meet them unaccompanied, and smoking drugs for half the night.

'We know your secret,' taunted Kayla-Jane.

I played dumb, my heart pounding. 'What secret?'

Frankie crawled out of the van and walked me away a few paces. I could see the bags under her eyes. She pointed a finger right into my face. 'Caleb,' she said.

'I've been going out with the Gorgias, that's all.'

Her voice became very direct. 'Do you know what me dad's going to do when he finds out?'

I couldn't swallow. I knew if that happened I would never see Caleb again.

'He'll move us away from here if he finds out you have Gorgia friends.'

Relief flooded over me. She didn't know we were more than friends.

'We'll have to cover for each other then,' I said calmly.

She shook my hand. 'It's a deal.' We held each other and she kissed my cheek.

'I love ya.'

'I love you too.'

As Frankie skipped back to the van, I made my way back to our trailer.

For several months after that, everything seemed to be going well. Frankie and I rarely saw each other, but if our mother or father asked, we had been together all evening. Then someone told our mother what Frankie was really up to, and she told our father.

They waited for Frankie that night, and discovered that I too was not in the trailer. We were both caught, and in between the shouting and the arguments and the threats, Frankie tried to deflect the attention from herself to me.

'Mikey's hanging about with a gay Gorgia man.'

When my mother turned and asked if that were true, I denied it, though my cheeks burned scarlet. I confessed that I had been hanging out with some people from the Dyna Bowl, but insisted that Caleb was not gay. My mother accepted this, but my father beat me until he was spent.

'If I *ever* hear anything like that around my ears again, I fucking swear I will kill you.'

Two days later we were moved as far away as my father could take us. And I was kept under tight watch until we left, so I didn't even have a chance to let Caleb know.

I was being taken from the one person in my life that had made me feel truly alive.

As we left the lanes of Newark, my insides caved in. I lay on the floor in the back of the van and felt myself die.

And yet I was still there. In that moment, that van and that life. My prison.

Two days later I managed to ring Caleb from a phone booth. We had been moved to a camp, miles away, in Chertsey.

He had been terribly worried that something had happened to me, and with no way to contact me, all he'd been able to do was wait in the retirement camp, night after night.

I burst into tears. 'It's no good,' I told him. 'I don't know when I will ever be able to see you again.'

'I'm not letting you go,' he said. 'I'll wait. We'll find a way, somehow.'

I promised to call him when I could, but I had no idea when that would be.

My father was determined to keep me from going anywhere. We went to work and once we came back, I wasn't allowed to leave my trailer.

The camp was full of married couples and families with young children. There were no young people my age at all. It was as though the clock had turned back, and the last year, with its new freedoms and friends, hadn't happened at all.

Frankie was distraught. She moped and sulked and spent most of her time in bed. But she too was using that phone booth. Wisdom tracked us down and within weeks she was once more sneaking out to meet him while the rest of the camp slept.

Frankie confided in our mother, who, realising that this was what her daughter wanted and that she wouldn't be stopped, gave her support and covered for her.

I was glad for Frankie, but it made me feel even worse, trapped in the trailer and unable to see Caleb at all. I managed to ring him a couple of times and he wanted to come and see me, but I wouldn't let him. I knew it was too dangerous – my father would have killed us both.

For the next couple of months, my father trailed around looking for work, finding very little. We were in a part of the country that had a big population of Gypsies, so the competition was fierce. And the lack of work put my father into a mood that darkened further each day. I turned fifteen, but this time there were no celebrations.

The only good thing about the Chertsey camp was that Frankie got in touch with our old friend Jamie-Leigh. Her family had come into a lot of money and her father had bought a huge house, just a few miles from the camp.

At nearly fifteen, Jamie-Leigh had chosen to become a born-again Christian, though it certainly didn't put her off cigarettes or alcohol, or curb her famous foul language. She was still utterly gorgeous and still had a mouth like a sewer.

Jamie-Leigh was one of the few people I was allowed to see and it was wonderful to hang out with her again. I always felt that we were soul-mates and she, Frankie and I began spending a lot of time together, walking through the camp, talking about our lives, laughing over our school-days and sharing our frustrations at out miserable, trapped lives as teenagers.

Our parents hoped they might be able to save us both by persuading us to marry and Jamie-Leigh dropped hints that I might ask her out. I loved her, as I always had, and if my life had been different, she would have been the only girl I could have married. But I was in love with Caleb, and even though I never wanted to hurt her, I ignored Jamie-Leigh's hints.

Work was so scarce that my father had to sell all of his jewellery, and swap his vehicles for an old pick-up and a dodgy Cortina. He fretted and worried and, after three months, he decided, with a bit of persuasion from my mother, that we should return to Newark. He had always found work there, he felt the place was lucky, and my mother convinced him that Frankie and I had learned our lessons and there would be no more sneaking out to meet Gypsy boys for her, or mixing with Gorgias for me.

Though it meant saying another sad goodbye to Jamie-Leigh, I was overjoyed to be going back. I knew that it would still be very dangerous to meet Caleb, so I called him to tell him I was coming back, but would still be under trailer arrest, and I had no idea when I might manage to see him again.

Once we arrived it was hard to resist the longing to run over to the retirement camp next door, in the hope that he would be waiting there for me, but I didn't dare.

I went to work each day with my father, and then spent the evenings sitting with my mother, Minnie and the boys. I would play with them until they went to bed, and then sit with my mother and talk.

Despite my frustrations and longing to be with Caleb, it was a special time.

My mother talked about her colourful childhood and shared stories with me as we went through her CDs and reminisced about the past. I loved the feeling of being close to her in a way that had rarely happened in the past. The two of us would sit up together until the men came home from the pub, when I would slip away to my trailer before my father came in. He still wasn't speaking to me, and my mother and I both thought it best for me to avoid him. We knew it was only a matter of time before the rage building up inside him would erupt.

After another month of boiling silence, it finally did.

We were gritting a driveway when my father decided I had been too slow shovelling the grit. He walked over, grabbed the shovel out of my hand and swung it across my face, knocking me over. He swung the shovel at me again and again, until finally he threw it down and carried on with the job. As I wept, one of the dossas came over to help me up, but my father ordered him to leave me exactly where I was. The dossa picked up the shovel and carried on from where I left off

When we got back home, my mother was horrified at the sight of me. She screamed at my father, who kicked Henry-Joe and Jimmy out of the trailer, telling them to go and play, then dragged her inside.

I was left standing outside, covered in grit and blood. And in that moment, I knew that this was it. I had to go. I ran down the lane, through the camp and towards the retirement camp next door, desperately hoping I would see Caleb's little orange pumpkin of a car.

As I turned the corner my heart leaped – it was there. He had come down after work to wait for me, as he had every day, in the hope that I would be able to sneak out. I opened the car door and got in, and we both burst into tears. The joy of finding one another again was muted by my fear, and Caleb's horror at the sight of my battered face.

Wiping his tears on his sleeve, he took off, and didn't stop driving until we had found a quiet side road in which to stop and talk.

I told him everything, including what Joseph had done to me, and my real age. And I told him I couldn't go on being around my father, or hiding who I really was.

Caleb listened, and then told me he had guessed I was far younger than I pretended to be, though he was shocked to find I was only fifteen.

'How did you know,' I asked.

'Because whenever we talked about the Gypsies getting married early, I wondered why you and your friends were not doing all of that yet. Besides, what twenty-year-old has curfews and still has to live by his father's rules?'

It was a good point. And it made me realise that if I remained there, I would never, ever escape my father. Not when I was twenty; not even when I was forty. I would never be what he wanted, and I would never leave his shadow. I could waste my whole life trying to win his approval and never succeed.

I had to accept that he would never change.

I told Caleb how desperate I felt.

'I know,' he said. 'That's why I'm going to take you away.'

He had a plan. He had been made manager of a Dyna Bowl up north, and he was leaving to begin his new job the following week. He asked me to wait two months, so that the Gypsies wouldn't link his going with mine, and then follow him. He would be waiting for me, and we would begin a new life together.

I was happy, excited – and scared. Could we really do

it? Could I face leaving my mother, Frankie, the boys and Minnie, knowing I might never see them again? It would break my heart.

But I had to go.

I had dreamed of escape so many times. But until now I'd had no idea how I would survive. Now I had someone who loved me, who would show me how to make a life for myself in the Gorgia world. Now the time was right.

When I got back to the camp an hour later, my absence hadn't even been noticed. My mother filled a bowl of hot water and passed it to me. She had a black eye and several large bruises. We looked at one another and held back our tears. And as I turned to walk over to my trailer, she rubbed my back. 'Clean that old bastard off you, my boy. I love you.'

It was only the second time I had ever heard her say it. I looked at her, and felt so much love. She had always done her best to fight for me. And now I was leaving her.

The day before Caleb left for his new job, I slipped out early and went to spend the day with him. I knew I would have to face my father's wrath when I returned, but it was worth it to spend a few precious hours together.

Caleb drove me back well before my father was due home from work. But he had second-guessed us, and was waiting.

I jumped out of Caleb's car and my father jumped into his and sped off after Caleb. I was terrified, but thankfully when my father returned an hour later, his black mood confirmed that he hadn't caught him.

I was beaten again, but I didn't care. Aching and bloody, I lay in my bunk and dreamed of my freedom.

For the next two months I carried on going to work with my father, and spent the evenings with my mother. I said nothing to her about Caleb or my feelings for him, but I knew that she knew there was someone. And she knew too that I was unhappy.

One evening Frankie slipped into the trailer, grinning. 'Guess what I did today?' she said.

'What?'

'I got married.'

I gasped. 'You married Wisdom?'

'Yes. I love him, Mikey, he's the one. I didn't want to wait any longer. We went to the Register Office in town and did it.'

I was shocked, and somehow saddened. I had imagined a big wedding for Frankie, with all the family there. And I wanted her to find a good husband. She was only ever going to have one chance, and I felt very afraid that she had blown it by sneaking off and marrying a low-life like Wisdom. But I said none of this.

'Congratulations, sis. I'm glad if you're happy.'

'I am,' she grinned. 'I'm going to find the right moment to tell Mum, and then she'll help me with Dad. Don't say a word to anyone yet.'

'Course I won't.'

A few days later I managed to slip out of camp to call Caleb. The two months were almost up, he was settled, and I didn't want to wait any longer. We agreed he would come for me a week later.

The day before I left was bright and hot and I looked on as my father trained seven-year-old Jimmy to fight. Déjà vu set in as I watched Jimmy begin to cry following a punch from my father. Smack, smack, smack; he hit him three more times.

I jumped from the trailer. 'Leave him alone,' I yelled.

As my father turned to beat me out of the way, both my mother and my sister stood up to him too.

'I swear to God, Frank, if you touch that boy again, I will kill you myself,' my mother screamed, angrier than I had ever seen her before.

My father drew back a hand to hit her.

'Go on then,' she screamed. 'I swear it, Frankie, I'll call the Gavvers (police) right now and have you put away for life.'

As the argument raged and Frankie joined in, I grabbed Henry-Joe and Jimmy and led them away.

We walked through the fields behind the camp, and I told them I was leaving. I wanted to let them know, so that they wouldn't wake and find me gone and think I hadn't cared about them. I told them that they were not to ever take the shit from our father that I had. Henry-Joe, at nine, was so mature; he understood the whole obsession our family had for fighting almost as well as I did. But he knew that his fight would be to protect Jimmy. The two of them were understanding, beautiful and innocent. I reached down and grabbed hold of them both, hugging them as tightly as I could.

'Your big brother loves you, don't forget that,' I whispered. 'And tell Minnie for me too, when she's old enough to understand.'

When we got back Aunt Minnie beckoned me over. My mother and father, Uncle Jaybus, Frankie and Romaine were all gathered together in Aunt Minnie's trailer, the row over Jimmy forgotten.

'Someone's here to fight you,' they chorused. I stepped inside the trailer.

'Who is it?'

'Davey Nelson,' Frankie said. I looked over to our plot and saw his van parked next to it.

'What should the boy do?' asked Aunt Minnie. 'He's a rough one.'

'I don't know,' said Romaine, peeking through the curtains.

Then they all piped up, telling me what to do, how to handle him, or to run away. But my father's voice was louder than all the others. 'If you don't beat this boy, I'll beat you all the way to Basingstoke.'

It was the same line I had heard him say when I was six years old in that boxing club and had heard over and over again ever since.

I opened the trailer door and marched out. My mother ran up behind me.

'Mikey, you don't have to face this boy if you don't want to do it.'

I looked at her. 'I'll be all right.'

I walked over to the parked van, and without giving the boy sitting inside the chance to make the challenge I opened the door and dragged him outside.

Suddenly it all flashed before me. The fights, the beatings, the put-downs and insults. And all those years of hating myself for this stupid sport.

I punched, and I punched, and I punched him over, and over, until I tore the skin from my knuckles and the blood from his face was all over my hands.

He hit the ground, and I stood back and waited for him to get up as the whole camp gathered round. He scrambled up from the floor, got back into his van, and was gone.

I had done it. This was the moment my father had waited for all these years. All he'd ever wanted was for his son to publicly beat the crap out of someone.

Suddenly, there was a different father standing in front of me. He beamed with pride, patting me on the back and trying to raise my arm like a champion. I pulled out of his grip and walked away.

I wasn't proud at all. All I could think of was what a waste of a life it was, beating the crap out of some bully, who deserved to be beaten by a better man than me.

I felt numb.

The following day it was raining. I packed a bag and then threw it from our trailer window into the back of the pick-up.

When I went outside I saw that our van was gone. My father saw me looking at the empty space.

'Your mum's gone to pick up some things from your granny Bettie's.'

After Granddad Tommy's death a few months ago Granny Bettie had settled into a bungalow half an hour's drive away.

I felt overwhelmed with sadness. I had wanted to see her just one more time. But I couldn't afford to wait. I hoped she would forgive me.

I grabbed the keys to the pick-up.

'Where are you going?' bellowed my father.

'Just going to ring Mum from the phone box,' I called.

'Be back in five minutes; you're still not allowed off this place and I need the motor,' he shouted.

My heart was skipping beats as I flew up the road to the phone box. When I reached it, I jumped from the pick-up, threw my bag into a hedge and put my last ten pence in the phone. Caleb had come back to Newark the night before and was waiting at his family's house for my call.

'Are you coming?'

'Yes,' I replied. 'Hurry.'

I put down the phone and drove back to the camp.

I pulled over in the pick-up, threw the keys on the table inside, and stood at the end of our plot. I could hear Romaine and Aunt Minnie, singing along to their Whitney Houston album as they cleaned out their trailers a few yards away. I waved to Frankie, as she and Kayla-Jayne walked over to the toilet block. Life as usual. But I would never see it again.

I waved to Frankie. I would miss her, but in some ways I felt I had lost her long ago. We were once so close, but she was no longer the best friend I played with when we were children. The influence of Wisdom, the late nights and the drugs had changed her so much. I didn't like what she had become, and I hoped that one day she would once again be the wonderful funny, kind-hearted girl she had once been.

I looked into my parents' trailer and saw my father engrossed in an old western on TV.

I turned and walked to the end of the camp and around the corner. Then I started to run. Suddenly I was running for my life; past the house where Adam used to live, under the trees, through the front camp and toward the gate. The wind whistled and slapped at my face as I picked up speed.

Then I heard my brothers call me. They came rushing towards me, covered in mud.

'Are you going now?' Henry-Joe asked.

I hugged them.

'I love you both, don't you ever forget that.'

Henry-Joe smiled. 'Look after yourself.' He sounded like a little man already.

'We'll be good,' said Jimmy.

We waved goodbye as I ran as fast as I could, up the road to where Caleb was waiting for me by the phone box. I dragged my bag from the hedge, threw it into the back of the car and jumped in as Caleb revved up and sped away.

I wiped the tears from my eyes. The road ahead was straight and clear. The sun had come out.

22

Today

I open my eyes and rub the sleep from them. A police siren screeches by as barking dogs skim through the grass in the park below my window. For a second I don't remember what day it is.

Today is my wedding day.

Across the room a neatly pressed suit hangs from a brass chandelier. And on the floor beneath it sits a pair of red-sequinned Converse sneakers. My ruby slippers.

I throw back the covers, get out of bed and walk three steps to the armchair. I sit and light a cigarette.

It is the morning after a storm. I sat up until three to listen to it, smoking and envying every Gypsy who still gets to hear the force of the rain as it dances across a trailer roof.

I stub out the cigarette and head for the shower. As I towel myself down, the phone rings. It is Belle, my best pal, and glamorous driver of the wedding car.

'Darling, you're getting married! How do you feel?'

I peer into the mirror. There is a red slash across my nose. I have injured myself in my sleep again.

'I look terrible.'

'Oh do fuck off, dear, you're gorgeous.'

'There's a cut on my nose. Do you have any make-up?'

I can hear her rummaging through her stacked bag.

'Mascara, foundation, lipstick . . .'

'Some good cover-up?'

'Got it. Don't you worry, today you are the beautiful groom, and I am Estée Lauder.'

She hangs up and I start to get ready.

I put on my candy-striped shirt, silver-blue suit and, lastly, the ruby slippers. They pinch my ankles, but I love them. They take me back to being four years old, prancing about the trailer in my aunt Minnie's red high-heels.

I am ready, but Belle won't be here for another half hour. I sit back in the armchair, and light another cigarette.

It is thirteen years since I climbed into Caleb's car and fled from my family and my people. It has been a long, tough journey, with twists and turns I could never have imagined.

I always believed that my future would be with Caleb, but I was wrong.

The day we escaped, he drove me to the home that he had found for us both in Manchester. It was the first night we had ever spent together. As I watched him sleep, I wanted so much to believe that everything would turn out right. But I knew better. Caleb loved me enough to steal me from my people, risk everything to have me with him and teach me how to live in his world. But I knew my people, and I knew what my father could be capable of if someone roused his anger. Caleb should have known better than to get caught up in a world of which he knew nothing. But I should have told him more about it. I was scared.

We were driving by Caleb's work when his phone rang, the next morning. Within twenty-four hours my father, along with several others, had tracked down Caleb's mother in Newark, burst into her house and torn it apart searching for me. My father had threatened her, warning her that he was going to find her son and me, and that he would be back every day until I was handed over.

No sooner had he left when she rang Caleb to warn him. She sounded so terrified as she cried down the receiver, begging him to do what my father said. But Caleb denied all knowledge of where I was, even to her.

From that moment on the phone didn't stop ringing. Like invaders, my father was hunting down every person that Caleb knew. Friends, family and people from his old job began to call, asking questions, warning him, and repeating what my father had said: 'That Gypsy boy's dad's just been in here', 'Do you know where Mikey Walsh is?', 'We know he's with you Caleb', 'Mikey's father is offering £100, just for your phone number'. Every call brought another fearful voice through the speaker in Caleb's car. My father was bribing, threatening and beating information out each and every one of them. Frightened people talked, and it wasn't long before my father came after us. Then someone actually took my father's money. He got a hold of Caleb's phone number.

To hear that man's voice at the other end of the phone terrified me. I had deluded myself into thinking that I would never hear that rumble of a voice ever again, and now he was calling every minute, demanding to know of Caleb's whereabouts and making threats toward his family to get him to agree to meet him. Caleb refused to tell him, and so the hunting continued, and it wasn't long before my father got the information he needed to find us.

We were sat in the car when I got the most sickening

feeling in my stomach. My body filled with fear and I began to lower myself down in the passenger seat. I could feel him. Seconds later, my father's van was coming towards us on the opposite side of the road.

I quickly ducked out of sight, but seeing Caleb, my father put up a chase. Caleb swore and shouted with fear as his little car careered down the narrow roads, managing to lose my father briefly, so that I could jump from the car and hide. I ran into in a pub, locking myself in a toilet cubicle, and stayed there until Caleb came back for me.

When he returned he was bloody and battered. He didn't need to tell me that my father had caught up with him. He left me at the pub while he went to his work to warn them not to answer any questions from anyone who came looking for him. And on his way there, the phone rang again. It was Henry-Joe.

He had stolen the phone from my father's coat pocket after lights out and in a whisper from his hiding place, Henry-Joe asked Caleb to send me home. Of course Caleb said nothing and assured Henry-Joe that I was not with him and he comforted my brother as he quietly cried into the receiver. Then Henry-Joe gave Caleb a warning that made his blood run cold: my father had put a contract out on me. He had spread the word among the travellers that I had stolen a valuable ring from him and offered a reward of ten thousand pounds to anyone who could bring this fictitious piece of jewellery back to him and break my legs, so that I could never run again.

As Caleb walked into the lobby, my mother was waiting for him. She had slipped out in secret to come and see him. My mother knew Caleb would not admit that he was hiding me, but told him, that if he did know where I was, we had to get away before they came for me.

Fearing for our safety, Caleb hid me and all my belongings in the boot of his car. In the middle of the night, a gang of travellers came for me and I listened from the boot as Caleb was beaten again, to force him to talk. For three more weeks I lived in his car boot and hid in churches, pubs and supermarkets for hours on end, while Caleb, beaten up over and over again, still refused to betray me.

It couldn't go on. One day after he had finished work, he picked me up from the pub he had left me in and drove me to Leeds, using a friend's car, so that we wouldn't be followed. He gave me fifty pounds and told me to find a bed and breakfast and look for a job. He was leaving his new job to go back to Newark, in an attempt to convince the Gypsies that he wasn't with me.

He took the number from a phone box next to the station, giving me the date and time when he would call, in one month's time.

I couldn't blame him for doing it. But at fifteen, I was standing on a street corner, with a bag and barely enough money to survive a few days. I was frightened, alone, and didn't know whether he would really come back.

I walked the streets, looking for a cheap place to stay, being turned away from door after door. Then a landlady took pity on me and took my fifty for one week's rent. All I had left was a few pence, which I used to buy a packet of instant mash. Three days into my first week I was so hungry that I passed out in the shower.

After that, I swallowed my pride, went out into the streets, and begged.

One day, I walked into a bar and was offered a cleaning job by a kind manageress. She even helped me to fill out the application form, since I could barely read or write.

Before I could be paid, I had to have a bank account. Plucking up my courage, I walked into a high street bank, sat down in front of the adviser and told her my whole story. She did something extraordinary, letting me use her address and helping me with the forms so that I could open an account.

Somehow I survived for two more weeks until my first pay cheque came in. After that, all I had left to do was wait for Caleb's call.

He called at exactly the time he had promised. I was tearful with relief to just hear his voice, and within days, he was coming up to see me again.

But Caleb's perception on what we had was changed forever. The pressure of the travellers, still calling on him daily, and my father's threats hanging over him and his family, were taking their toll. He couldn't take it any longer. Every time he came to visit, there was a new injury and a new threat. Endless phone calls from strangers threatening to break Caleb's legs made him change his phone and not tell anyone the number. Not even his own family. Caleb was falling into a deeply paranoid state that began to distort his feelings for me. Not knowing his number did not stop his torture. Gypsies were still coming to his house and following him to and from his work. My father had set the price and now all he had to do was sit back, while those in need of the money would do the searching for him.

Finally he cracked, turning on me, and I had to say goodbye.

At sixteen years old, I was alone in the Gorgia world. I

had lost Caleb, and could not go back to my home even if I had wanted to.

There was no turning back.

I carried on with my job in Leeds for a few months. Once a month I would write a letter to my mother, taking a train to a different place each time to post it, so that I couldn't be traced. Sometimes I would make a day of it, finding a nice café or pub in a strange town to sit and write and choosing the perfect place to post it.

My letters were all written phonetically, and all in capitals. I knew my mother would be able to read them, because I wrote just the way she always had done. And I posted the letters to her at Granny Bettie's bungalow.

After saving enough money, I moved to Liverpool and took a job in a gay bar. I found new friends, and met Leigh. We became the best of friends and moved in together.

In between shifts, I began to educate myself. I read many books and learned new words every day, lapping up a world I had been denied as a child.

I saw plays and films and discovered the world of the theatre. And with Leigh's help I got a place on a theatre education course. Two years later I auditioned for the Guildhall School of Music and Drama in London. When I heard that I had got in, and would be moving south in a few months time, I was astonished, thrilled, and proud.

I was finally making a life for myself.

But I missed my mother. I couldn't go through a day without thinking of her, my sisters and the boys.

Five years after we had last met, I wrote to my mother, telling her the truth about my sexuality and my lifestyle. I told her I would understand if she never wanted to see me again, but that I hoped she would come and meet me. I gave two dates, two locations and two times, in case she couldn't make the first. I knew there was always a risk that my father might find out and follow her. But my longing to see her was bigger than my fear.

The first location I'd given was at a city centre hotel. I waited for thirty minutes on the front steps, with no sign of her. My heart broke, as I convinced myself that I would have to go on without ever having her back in my life. Then, there was the hoot of a car horn.

I looked up and saw her, sitting in a small white van, beside the curb. As our eyes met, we both burst into tears. I jumped from the steps, pulled open the van door and threw my arms around her.

'I love you, my Mikey,' she sobbed. 'I love you. I knew, I always knew, you know, and I didn't care. You were special, you were my little boy.'

I was shocked. She knew? I felt I'd just heard that I'd had the power to go back to Kansas all along.

She was still the wonderful, celestial woman I remembered. The smell of ground coffee and lipstick filled my senses as I breathed her in.

She turned to the back seat of the van, and picked up a big bundle of letters – hers to me, for the day when she would be finally able to give them to me. All, like mine, written phonetically, and in capital letters. There were Christmas cards, birthday cards and the presents she had bought and kept hidden under her bed over the past five years. She had never given up hoping.

I took her for lunch, and then to my flat, where she met Leigh. The three of us laughed and reminisced for several hours, until she had to leave, to get back home before my father returned from work.

She told me that Frankie had confessed her marriage to Wisdom once she became pregnant. She had moved onto a convoy with his family. When she was eight months pregnant, she stole twenty pence from Wisdom's pocket and ran away as he slept. She called our mother, who came to collect her and took her home. A month later Frankie gave birth to a baby boy. She called him Frank.

At just eighteen Frankie was divorced and condemned to live with her parents, bringing up her son, alone. According to Gypsy custom, no man would ever look at her again.

When we parted, my mother said she was going to go home and tell my father she was in touch with me again and that he had better accept it. And she said she would come again and bring Frankie, Henry-Joe, Jimmy and Minnie.

To my amazement, she did. We met in a local airport – her idea because, although she was scared stiff of flying, she loved watching the planes.

As I walked the long white tunnel into the terminal, I saw Henry-Joe standing at the window. He turned and looked at me before shouting my name and running toward me. He had been a child when I last saw him, but the boy charging down the tunnel with his arms flung wide was bigger than me. He jumped on top of me and we hugged and cried and laughed.

Behind him came Jimmy, now twelve years old, a hulking lad, the living image of our father. Running after him was Minnie, seven years old, and the spitting image of our mother. Then there was Frankie, grinning at me and holding an adorable baby. My nephew. My mother was with them, and beside her – to my shock and amazement – was my father.

For a moment the old fear returned, but he greeted me with respect, shaking my hand and patting my back, before graciously taking a step back to allow the rest of us to have time with each other and I realised that he had called a truce, if only for this day.

After five years in the wilderness, I had my family back.

We spent a couple of hours catching up, and after that day I was able to phone my mother regularly and she would pass me over to Frankie and the other three children to catch up. My father didn't come on the phone, nor did he agree to allow another meeting. But at least I had contact.

One afternoon, a few months later, Henry-Joe called me. He was worried. He had heard rumours about Uncle Joseph.

Henry-Joe said he was worried that he might be over-reacting, but he couldn't help suspecting something awful. He asked if I could help. He passed the phone to our mother and I asked her if I could come and visit.

'I'll see what your dad says, Mikey, but I'm sure we can make him say yes.' I packed a case and caught a train to West Sussex. My father had just bought an old farm there and was planning to turn it into a reputable Gypsy camp.

When the train pulled in I was shocked to see Joseph waiting for me. The sight of him made me nauseous. In my years away I had managed to forget what he had put me though, and refused even to give him a thought.

I played it cool, and greeted him. He decided to take us for a drive before heading to the house, and told me he had been worried about me. 'Why did you go, Mikey?'

I decided I'd tell him the truth, thinking it might get him to open up. 'I'm gay, Uncle Joseph.'

He looked at me for a moment; then sighed. 'I am too . . . and I love you.' His voice became desperate. 'I've been waiting for you to come home. I'm doing really well now. The yard is mine and I own my own funeral business. You could move in with me. No one will know and you'll never have to work again.'

'No, Uncle Joseph, I can't do that.'

He replied as if I had insulted him. 'Why not?'

'Because you're my uncle. And I don't feel the way you do.'

'But you used to.'

'No, *Joseph, I never, ever did.*'

I boiled with shame and fury. I wanted to kill him. It was almost unbearable to pretend to be friendly. But I knew that I had to bide my time.

My father's farmhouse was no more than the shell of a building, standing in a muddy yard. My mother had big dreams for it, but in the meantime they were living in two trailers: Frankie and baby Frankie in one, and the boys, Minnie, my mother and father in the other. I smiled to see that the god-awful awning was still fluttering gently in the breeze in front of my parents' trailer.

The boys, Minnie and Frankie were excited to see me, but my father just turned away. My mother had phoned, begging me not to let him know the truth about me. She told me that she was happy that I was being true to myself, but that my father would never see it the same way. If he ever found out, she and the kids would be the first to suffer. I promised her to keep it a secret.

That evening, as my father and Jimmy rolled around in fits of laughter in front of the movie *Home Alone*, I took my mother, Minnie and Henry-Joe over to Frankie's trailer.

As Frankie put the baby and Minnie to bed, I told them the whole truth about Joseph. As we spoke, Frankie's eyes widened with anger and our mother's face turned from white to fierce red. She asked that we all say nothing until she decided what she was going to do next.

The next morning I went into town with Henry-Joe. When we got back, the family were sitting on the outside deck furniture my father had stolen from a local pub.

My father leaped up, rushed over to me and punched me in the mouth.

'Frank stop!' screamed my mother as she, Henry-Joe and Jimmy prised him off me.

My father shook himself and stepped back. 'You poisonous little poof. How dare you come back here and spread stuff like that? Joseph is your uncle and thinks the world of you.'

I took my phone from my pocket. 'Let me phone him, and you'll hear how much he thinks of all of us.'

My father roared with fury and refused point blank.

'You won't do it, because you're frightened it's true,' my mother yelled.

My father shut his mouth and sank onto the bench, lighting a cigarette. My mother and Frankie calmed him and eventually he agreed to go into Frankie's trailer with me, to hear for himself.

Joseph answered after one ring. I turned the phone to speaker mode.

'Hello, my babe,' he said.

My father's face drained, but he remained silent.

'Joseph?' I said.

'Yes?'

I was terrified but I looked at my family gathered round the phone and took a deep breath. I had to do this. So I told Joseph that I had heard the rumours and knew they were true, and I told him what the years of abuse had done to me.

'But I *love* you, I've always loved you . . .' Joseph bleated.

I wondered if my father remembered the day I tried to tell him about Joseph, when I was a little boy.

As Joseph went on talking, my father's face visibly aged with shock.

'Joseph, if you come near this family ever again, I will kill you.'

'Mikey, please, don't talk to me like that.' Joseph began to sob. 'I love you, I've waited for you. Mikey, please! Say something . . .'

My father began to weep. I put down the phone then leaned over and placed my hand on my father's knee. I saw me in him for the first time in my life. But after a few seconds he pulled away, lifting his face from his palms to stare at me.

'Get out.'

A month later my mother called to say that my grandfather, Old Noah, was on his deathbed. And he wanted to see me.

My mother told me he had asked to see her alone. He asked her to empty out his pockets. She found a wad of fifty-pound notes, a pair of owl-eye glasses and a wallet with Granny Ivy's picture inside.

'Bettie, you have always done the right thing,' he told her. 'And I know that you and my Prissy have been best friends since you were babies.' He stretched out a shaky hand, heavy with gold rings. 'Take those things from my jacket and these rings and give them to Prissy. Otherwise as soon as I'm gone they'll pull them from my fingers and my little girl will end up with nothing.'

My mother did as he said, wiping his tears as she helped him remove the jewels from each finger.

'He says he's going to wait for you,' she said. 'Can I send someone to pick you up from London? He hasn't got much time left.'

I had no idea why my grandfather had asked for me. But I wanted to say goodbye. My mother sent her brother Alfie to collect me and we raced through the outskirts of London and onto the motorway. An hour later, as I ran through the hospital corridors towards his bedside, my grandfather died.

I sat beside him. His face was bruised from a fall and his weight had plummeted so low that he was barely recognisable. His left arm was in a bandaged sling that hung in the air. After such a heroic life and a major heart operation, it was a mere splinter, trapped under his fingernail that had finally done for him, causing an infection that spread through his body.

The king was dead. I would never look into those steely blue eyes again. And I would never know what he had wanted to say to me, but I often imagined, in the years after he died, that he had wanted to say he was proud of me.

I held his heavy hand in mine and sang my childhood party piece, 'Ol' Scotch Hat'. He'd always loved it.

His funeral, a few days later, was a huge affair. He had requested that his grandsons carry his coffin, but my father and Tory refused to allow me to take part.

'If he can't carry that coffin, then he will push me along right behind it,' Aunt Prissy said. And I did. There were more than a few hisses in my direction as I pushed her wheelchair through the crowd, and I kept my head down. But Aunt Prissy leaned back and looked me in the eyes. 'You've done better than any of these misfits, my boy. Not a one of them could ever do what you have done. You should be proud.'

Belle calls. She is stuck in traffic. I go out onto the balcony. The sun is warm and I turn my face to it. I look down at my shoes and tap them together. The sunlight blisters across the sequins, sending patterns of red against the wall.

I wish I could go back, just for a day, to play with Frankie, Jamie-Leigh, Olive and Twizzel, to thank Mrs Kerr for making me feel I wasn't useless, to see my little grandmother combing Aunt Prissy's beautiful hair. To try again with my father.

But I can't go back, and I'm proud of where I am today.

I moved to London with Leigh, both of us convinced that it would surely bring us both the fame and fortune we so rightly deserved.

Over White Russians, we clinked our glasses to the idea that London would be the place to grow up, rehabilitate and finally use our experiences to get creative. He took up a course in creative writing, and I had my hard-won place at drama school.

I loved every crazy creative minute of it. Three years of

soaking up knowledge, friendship, and a sanctuary where I could release all my inner angst. I learned the joy of expressing myself through creative writing and finally got, and loved, Shakespeare. In that school I found people I knew I would be close to for the rest of my life.

After it was all over, the idea of walking on stage was no longer important. I tried the acting thing, but I only lasted a few months. I hated the idea of auditioning: the strangers, the casting calls, the constant need to please and be liked . . . and then the pain of rejection. It was a relief to walk away.

In between the crappy acting jobs I had worked in a bar. It became a great refuge, and a place I will always hold close to my heart. It was there that I made my closest friends, and met the man I'm marrying today.

I decided I wanted to work with children, getting a job as a teaching assistant, helping children with special needs. I smile sometimes to think how much most Gypsies hate schools, and here I am, spending my working life in one, and feeling so at home.

I learn all the time; about history, how our bodies work, where places are in the world. All the things I missed, first time around.

But Leigh is dead.

'I want a good life Mikey, not a long one,' he would always say.

The last time we met, we spent several hours reminiscing about the fun we'd had. Unsurprisingly for him, with his flair for melodrama, he brought up the subject of his death.

'We'll have an ending like that bit in *Beaches*. You can give me a big cuddle and tell me how jealous you've always been of me,' he laughed. 'And you can give me a big speech that makes everybody cry before they lift me out of the coffin and have me explode with glitter all over the audience.'

He wanted this moment to come at the crescendo of Nessun Dorma.

When he left the bar, we didn't have a big emotional goodbye. No big hug, kiss, or I love you. Just 'see you later'.

The next time I saw him it was our *Beaches* moment.

He had gone to a club and met a guy who had spiked his drink with a massive amount of liquid Ecstasy. Hours later he was in a coma and when I reached his bedside in hospital he could not speak or move. But he could cry, and he managed to squeeze my hand.

I hugged him just as he said I would. And told him how jealous of him I was, just as he said I would. And at his funeral I gave an eulogy to end all eulogies. Just as he said I would.

Then I came home and broke my heart.

My best friend was gone. All of our memories were now mine alone.

I still find myself trapped within rooms in my subconscious that I cannot understand. And I still have the odd nightmare and sleepless night and daily dose of self-doubt.

But who doesn't?

I don't as often as I did before. And when I sat down to write my story, it was as a tribute to Leigh, because without him I could never have done it.

A few months ago I attended Henry-Joe's wedding. Layla had been with us at Newark. He had grown up with her and now, over ten years later, they were to be husband and wife.

I had to be there to see the happiest day of his life. My

father was there, so I stood discreetly amongst the crowd, but that was good enough for me. I watched Henry-Joe spinning around the dance floor with his beautiful new wife and my mother's proud smiles and felt truly happy.

The day after Dillan said yes, I called Henry-Joe to ask him to be my best man. Only first, I had to come out to him. I asked how well he knew me, and he replied, pretty well.

I said I had something to tell him, and he said that he thought he already knew. I told him I was gay and he said, 'I love you even more for it.'

The next question was 'Will you be my best man?'

After several moments of shouting with surprise, he wept with joy. 'More than anything, Mikey, I would love to be your best man.'

Henry-Joe would be there for me, but my mother would not. If my father knew I was marrying, he would forbid my mother to come, and she could not bring herself to betray him. But she wanted to do something for us as a gesture of her love, so she made our wedding cake. Despite having been the world's worst cook throughout my childhood, she had since mastered the art of making a perfect fruitcake. And her passion for creative decor had evolved into an ability to make practically anything imaginable out of a roll of icing and a couple of well-placed toothpicks. So talented was she, that she had started her own cake-making business.

She made mine over a weekend when my father was away and I went to stay with her. We were up till all hours, designing, preparing, baking and sugar crafting. We moulded and nattered from dawn to dusk, and then from dusk till morning, taking only short coffee breaks in which I would draw up a picture of the 'bling' wedding ring I had made for Dillan and make her laugh with stories of him parading around in it.

The cake was a work of art which even my mother, whose cake-making skills had become renowned, was amazed to have accomplished. Three tiers high, and like a ghostly ball gown, with folds of shimmering white-chocolate icing. She crafted bouquets of edible flowers that burst from each ruffle. And at the very top, a solid white chocolate skull, covered in exotic flowers and strings of edible pearls. The people in the bar where we were holding our reception were in total awe of such a cake, when Henry-Joe and I dropped it off.

Before I left that weekend, my mother pulled me to one side and passed me a small green box. Inside she had put her own wedding ring.

'It's for you, Mikey. I want you to have it.'

It will be the one I wear on my finger today. I check the box to see it's still there.

The phone goes.

'Whooooo! I'm here!'

'Oh my God, Frankie?'

'Yes. I'm coming with Henry-Joe. And I'm wearing the biggest and brightest yellow dress you've ever seen!'

Just a month ago, full of half-cut confidence, I came out to her over the phone.

Her reaction was very different to the one I had from Henry-Joe. She said that she was angry that I could have kept such a secret from her all these years, and that she was happy for me, but could not take part in my life.

I hadn't expected to hear from her today, let alone see her.

She whoops into the phone, like a crazy ladette.

'Mikey, I've dyed my hair like Pamela Anderson! I'm a big fuckin' mermaid.'

I laugh out loud at the vision.

'You'll be the belle of the ball!'

'I know that ... don't think I haven't planned to find myself a rich husband there.'

After a few minutes of giving directions to the town hall, we hang up and I dance around the floor in bliss. How wonderful to have my brother as my best man, and Frankie there too.

Belle texts me that she has arrived and I go down to meet her. As I walk out of the door I see her standing on the open roof of her little 1950s convertible. She's wearing a vintage gold Moschino dress that makes her look just like Audrey Hepburn, only with massive knockers.

When I am three feet away, she honks on the horn and waves as if I was the other end of the park. Brightly coloured balloons float up from her car and into the clear blue sky, like a school of tropical fish.

We sit in the car and Belle slaps her miracle concealer across my nose. She turns the rear-view mirror towards me, so that I can check out her handiwork.

'Amazing,' I grin.

She snaps her compact shut and winks. 'Told you.'

We set off down the road, launching several more balloons as we roar along. With the wheel in one hand, and her satnav in the other, Belle leans over and grabs a cigarette from my carton with her teeth.

As I light her up and grab my own, Henry-Joe calls again. They are in the bar across from the town hall. I tell them I will only be a few minutes.

A text arrives from my mother.

'Good luck, my son. I love you with all my heart.'

We stop briefly at the bar where the reception will be, so that I can take the foil off the cake. My lovely, and always reliable mate Rufus is there, the perfect master of ceremonies organising everything. The bar looks incredible; all wooden panels, fairy lights, exotic flowers and pastel-coloured birds.

Back in the car Belle looks at me.

'This is it.'

As we drive, I plug my iPod into the stereo. The wind sweeps through Belle's hair as we sail toward the town hall and I think of Caleb. I will always love him. I wonder about where he is now, what he is doing and whether he would be happy for me. I hope he is happy.

With five minutes to go before the ceremony, Belle pulls over in front of the pub opposite the town hall. She leans over and kisses me.

'See you inside, my darling.'

She flies off in a mass of balloons, as a crowd of brightly coloured gowns, frock coats, top hats and layers of sparkles spill out of the pub, all cheering.

There are my friends from Liverpool, from the Guildhall, and the wonderful little bar where I first met Dillan; a decade of new and old friends. And beside them, smiling proudly, stand my brother, his wife Layla, and my sister.

Like an elegant circus they all parade across to the town

hall, hugging me, shaking my hand, and blowing kisses, wishing me luck as they pass.

Last of all comes Dillan, in his white Vivienne Westwood suit and silver trainers.

We stand and grin at one another.

Frankie spins round, her dress cracking like a dragon's tail in the middle of the road.

'Hurry up, then!' she laughs.

We race to catch up with our merry band, crossing the road and winding its way up the marble steps toward the great oak doors.

Epilogue

Two years after my father learned the truth about Joseph, he turned up at Joseph's door with Jimmy and let him know that he knew the truth. Joseph lashed out at my father, but Jimmy, by then in his mid teens and as large as a truck, punched him in the mouth, exploding four of his front teeth.

Four more boys came forward to say that Joseph had also abused them. Unwilling to pass him over to the police, the accusing boys' fathers, their friends and relatives made his last years a living hell. He was hunted, tortured, and beaten up by men who once looked up to our family. He went to work for a scrap company in another town, and five years ago he died, alone in his home, from a heart attack.

My father no longer has anything to do with his remaining brother, Tory. After Old Noah died, Tory refused to speak to them again, and in the following years, he lost most of his money.

My father has throat cancer – a legacy of his years of heavy smoking. He is near blind, and spends most of his time asleep in front of the TV. His last attempt at bullying the family ended when Henry-Joe stood up to him and hit him back, yelling 'You might be able to scare everyone else, old man, but I am not a little boy any more. I'm a better man than you will ever be, so don't ever raise your hand to me again.'

My father did not. He knew that he had been beaten.

Jimmy, now barely twenty, turned out to be the wolf my father had hoped for. But my father's violent training back-fired. No one, not even my father, can stop Jimmy's violence now. My father came to believe he was possessed, and took him to a church in the hope of an exorcism. It made no difference: Jimmy still spends his life looking for trouble. He has been charged several times with grievous bodily harm – on one occasion, towards thirteen people at one time. It began as a spat in the local pub when a Gorgia man tried to chat up Frankie. She tried to get rid of him before Jimmy arrived back from the bar. She pushed him away and he punched her in the eye in front of Jimmy, sealing his doom. The night ended with several people with broken bones and the guy who started it all with his index finger bitten off by Jimmy and spat across the carpet.

The days of knocking on doors are history – it is now against the law to call, the way Gypsies used to. The younger generation, while determined to carry on with their traditions for as long as possible, are having to find new ways of surviving.

I hope that they can. Left to themselves the Romanies live peacefully and quietly, away from the spotlight. But the Irish Travellers have damaged the image of travelling people everywhere – parking trailers wherever they choose, and scattering litter. There is also a lot more violence, not just with fists, but with knives.

A couple of years ago my brothers were accosted by a gang of fifteen Irish Travellers, aware of the reputation of our family as fighters. Henry-Joe and Jimmy were prepared to fight, but knives appeared, and today Henry-Joe has vicious scars across his back, and Jimmy, after surgery for wounds to his face, was left with paralysed muscles down one side.

As for our old friends, many of them have encountered hard times.

Kayla-Jayne's boyfriend Tyrone left her after she slept with him. Weeks later she realised she was pregnant. She kept it hidden until the eighth month, when her family found out. Tyrone was forced to marry her, but of course it didn't last, and, like Frankie, she and her child live with her parents.

Levoy turned to crack not long after my departure, and was sent to stay with a family in San Diego to dry out. I saw him a few years ago, and although he was free of drugs, they had affected him deeply, both physically and mentally. He now lives with his parents and works in a local store in Newark. Bitter about what our upbringing has made him, he doesn't see any of the people he used to know.

Adam came back to the Newark camp, and is now married, with three children.

Romaine didn't marry. Now in her mid-twenties, she is regarded as a spinster. Aunt Minnie still wears her fur coat.

Jamie-Leigh married a violent man, who, while high on Ecstasy, was hit by a train and killed. In the years after I left Newark, when both she and Frankie had lost their husbands and were excluded socially, they found one another again and became very close. Jamie-Leigh would come round every day, always joking with my brothers that she was waiting for me to return and marry her. When my family came to meet me at the airport she had sent with them a paper napkin, with a large heart drawn on it to give to me. Underneath she had written, with perfect spelling, 'I love you'.

Soon after that, Jamie-Leigh got involved with the underworld and began smuggling drugs. She was caught with cocaine strapped to her thighs, and is now serving a long sentence in a South American prison. I don't know if we will ever meet again, but I will always feel she is a part of me.

My cousin Tory got married and lives with his wife and children in a house across the way from Granny Bettie. Noah is divorced and works as a bodyguard now.

Aunt Maudie had a stroke while she cleaned the kitchen, and Uncle Tory came home that night to find her dead on the kitchen floor. He was devastated.

It breaks my heart to know how many of our people are struggling, and turning to drugs or crime. A once proud race has been brought to its knees.

And what of the mythical King of the Gypsies?

The real truth is that there never has been a Romany king. Only the odd self-proclaimed fool, who ends up getting himself and his whole bloodline beaten to a pulp.

I wouldn't change my life. If I hadn't done all that I have done, I wouldn't be where I am today. I am proud of my race, and what I am.

You can take the boy away from the Gypsies, but you can't take the Gypsy out of the boy.